Lella and Massimo Vignelli
Two Lives, One Vision

Lella and Massimo Vignelli
Two Lives, One Vision

Jan Conradi

RIT Press
Rochester, New York

Lella and Massimo Vignelli: Two Lives, One Vision

All images are used with permission. Unless otherwise noted,
the images were selected from the Vignellis' personal collection.
Cover photo © Dean Kaufman. Used by permission.
Cover: The Vignellis in their New York home, 2007.

RIT Press
90 Lomb Memorial Drive
Rochester, NY 14623
ritpress.rit.edu

Printed in the U.S.A.

ISBN 978-1-939125-07-1 (softcover)
ISBN 978-1-939125-08-8 (e-book)

Library of Congress Cataloging-in-Publication Data

Conradi, Jan, 1959– author.
    Lella and Massimo Vignelli : two lives, one vision / Jan Conradi.
        pages   cm
    Includes bibliographical references and index.
        ISBN 978-1-939125-07-1 (alk. paper) — ISBN 978-1-939125-08-8 (e-book)
1. Vignelli, Massimo. 2. Vignelli, Lella. 3. Designers—United
States—Biography. I. Title.
    NK1535.V53C66 2014
    745.4092'2--dc23
                                                                    2014018146

**Lella and Massimo Vignelli
Two Lives, One Vision**

For my mom and for family
who love and care
even when they do not understand

'55/'60

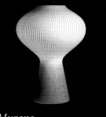

Venini, Murano

Venini, Murano

ni, Murano

Venini, Murano

'60/'65

Piccolo Teatro, Milan

Sansoni Books, Italy

'65/'70

r, New York

Poltronova, Milan

Subway signs, New York

Knoll International, USA

l International, USA

American Airlines, USA

Heller, New York

Industrial Design Magazine, USA

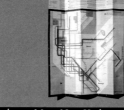

Subway Map, New York

Knoll International, USA

Bloomingdale's, New York

Heller, USA

Museum of Fine Art, Minneapolis

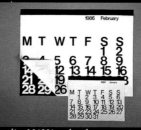

Stendig, NAVA calendars

'75/'80

1976 Bicentennial, USA

National Parks Service, USA

IAUS, New York

Hauserman, USA

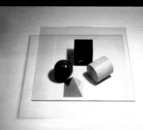

Casigliani, Italy

Chanticleer Press, New York

Heller, USA

'80/'85

'70/'75

The Herald, New York

...er, USA

San Lorenzo, Italy

San Lorenzo, Italy

Saint Peter's Church, New York

Saint Peter's Church, New York

...PPOSITIONS

...PPOSITIONS

...ositions Magazine, USA

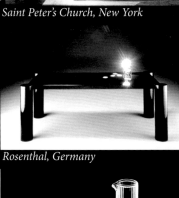

Rosenthal, Germany

Rosenthal, Germany

...Hotels, Italy

Ciga Hotels, Italy

Alfred A. Knopf, USA

...JY, New York

Knoll International, USA

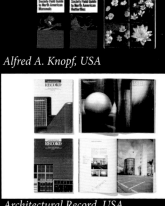

Architectural Record, USA

Rizzoli, New York

Harper & Row, New York

Parsons School of Design, New York

Acerbis International, Italy

Casigliani, Italy

Casigliani, Italy

Vignelli Office, New York

Vignelli Office, New York

Vignelli Office, New York

Acerbis International, Italy

Street Supergraphics, New York

Artemide Showroom, New York

Poltrona Frau, Tolentino

Poltrona Frau, Italy

Sasaki, Japan

AIA, Washington, D.C.

Fodor's Guides, USA

'90/'95

enter, Chicago

Hauserman, Los Angeles

Cleto Munari, Italy

'85/'90

ll International, USA

elli Office, New York

Vignelli Office, New York

Vignelli Office, New York

mide Showroom, New York

Poltrona Frau, Milan

Poltrona Frau, Tolentino

ki, Japan

Sasaki, Japan

Palio, New York

Cosmit, Italy

Fassati Wine, Italy

Prato Museum, Italy

AIUS, New York

American Center, Paris

Design:Vignelli, New York

Design:Vignelli, New York

Pierre Junod, Switzerland

'95/2000

Benetton, Italy

Poltrona Frau, Italy

Ducati Motors, Italy

SeaCat Ferry, London

Italian Railway Signs

Italian Railway Signs

Italian Railway Signs

2000/'05

San Lorenzo, Italy

Guggenheim, New York

Steelcase, USA

Poltrona Frau, Italy

rias, Spain

Faraone, Italy

San Lorenzo, Italy

ld Trade Center, Amsterdam

Guggenheim, Bilbao

Guggenheim, Bilbao

Guggenheim, Bilbao

ER, UK

GNER, UK

Termini Station Signs, Rome

eum of Fine Arts, Houston

Museum of Fine Arts, Houston

Museum of Fine Arts, Houston

Feudi di San Gregorio, Italy

Feudi di San Gregorio, Italy

Seaman Schepps Exhibit, New Yo

2005...

San Lorenzo, Italy

Taschen, Germany

Rizzoli, New York

MoMA, New York

Formica, USA

BK Italia, Italy

BK Italia, Italy

CorpGroup, Santiago

MTA, New York

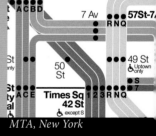

MTA, New York

Feudi di San Gregorio, Italy

Feudi di San Gregorio, Italy

Richard Meier, New York

...trona Frau, Milan

Poltrona Frau, Milan

Poltrona Frau, Verona

...hard Meier, New York

AAA, Dominican Republic

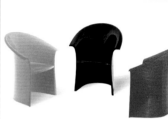

Heller, USA

...ges Publishing, Australia

Images Publishing, Australia

Lars Müller, Switzerland

...ibrahim, Turkey

Abdibrahim, Turkey

A Casa, Italy

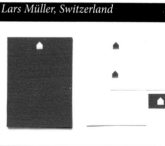

6 Restaurant, New York

SD26 Restaurant, New York

SD26 Restaurant, New York

...lworths, South Africa

MTA App, New York

Vignelli Center, Rochester

Foreword

Rather than make an argument for the importance of Lella and Massimo Vignelli's work, in this book, Jan Conradi has written an intimate and affectionate portrait of two gifted and remarkable people. The likely audience will have no need of any words of mine to convince them of the significance of the Vignellis and their role in the evolution of design over the last half century. They, like me, will have been depressed by the willful vandalism perpetrated by American Airlines when it obliterated the simple authority of its own Vignelli-designed livery. They, like me, remember the clarity and authority of the shortlived New York City subway diagram, a victim of the literalism of those who insisted on interpreting it as a map. With its glorious citrus fruit salad of colour and its supremely confident typography, it seemed to define modern New York with a thread of lucidity that ran throughout the decrepit system of the 1970s as a sign of better times to come.

In my study, I keep one personally resonant Vignelli-designed artifact. It's a copy of *Skyline,* the magazine published in New York in the late 1970s and early 1980s that mixed a tabloid format with a strong graphic language and high-culture content that inspired a group of us in London to set up *Blueprint.* Of course it set rather a worrying precedent by suspending publication shortly before we launched.

Conradi addresses the Vignellis' lives both in Europe, and in the US. The transatlantic connection is important to understanding them. Unlike the German refugees of the 1930s that Tom Wolfe mocked as the silver princes whom superstitious Americans got down on their knees to worship on their arrival from the Bauhaus, the Vignellis represented a different kind of Europe. And they had a different relationship with America.

Mies and Gropius took Europe to America in their suitcases. Massimo and Lella Vignelli were from another generation. They were Italian. And they went to America because they wanted to, not because they had to. They liked what they found there, in spite of themselves. In the 1960s, leftist Italians—

among whose number Massimo certainly counted himself—were not meant to be impressed by the vulgar materialism of the beating heart of American capitalism.

But then modern Italy has a way of accommodating such contradictions. Aldo Rossi, Massimo Vignelli's friend from their student days in Venice, was both a Marxist and prepared to work for Disney. The billionaire publisher Giacomo Feltrinelli—a client of Unimark's during Vignelli's time—was a revolutionary socialist who owned a yacht equipped with an elegantly uniformed crew.

The Vignellis brought this ambiguity to America with them. Helvetica, it sometimes seemed, was almost enough to bring moral salvation to the most black-hearted and anonymous corporate clients.

Massimo and Lella came to maturity as designers in postwar Italy, a society that between 1945 and 1965 went through a transformation that was the closest Europe has come to China's explosive growth of the last twenty years. What had been a largely pre-industrial economy—for all that Fiat and Olivetti achieved—tore through a phase as a producer of low-cost generic manufacturing, and then Italy embarked on reinventing itself as the world's center for contemporary design-led production. And unlike the German modernists of the 1930s, the Italian version of the 1950s and '60s came with a certain sensuous elegance that for all Massimo Vignelli's puritanical-sounding pronouncements, certainly infuses the Vignellis' work.

They emerged from the small and intense world of northern Italy, between Milan and Venice, full of talented architects and designers whose careers were interwoven. Both Massimo and Lella set out to be architects. It was a training that was the starting point for almost all of Italy's designers in the post-war years: Bellini, Magistretti, and Sottsass all went to architecture school, even if they did not become best known for their architecture.

In Milan, Massimo worked in the Castiglioni brothers' studio. He moved to Venice after graduating from the Brera Art Academy and a year of study in the architecture program at Politecnico di Milano. Lella studied in Venice too. She was a Valle, the sister and daughter of distinguished architects. She was taught among others by Franco Albini, who with his partner Franca Helg, was the architect of the first stations on the Milan metro, for which Bob Noorda, Massimo's partner at Unimark, created the identity system that got the Vignellis involved with the New York subway.

Massimo did not complete his studies (though he was later awarded an honorary degree). His sense of precision and order has perhaps its clearest expression in two, rather than three dimensions: in the field of graphic communication. Lella's sensibility has been in the exploration of tactile, material qualities. It can be seen in the use of the polished stucco, familiar in Venetian interiors, as the finish for the legs for the Serenissima glass-topped table she designed for Acerbis. She created a sequence of interiors for, among other clients, Poltrona Frau, that are in themselves exquisite as spaces, but also serve to make everything in them exquisite.

What really stands out from the Vignellis' body of work that it was simultaneously so diverse in its range and so consistent in its realisation. The survival instincts of the Italian design world and the lack of specialization there made it natural for the Vignellis to be as impressive in handling type and identity as furniture, glass and interiors. And all of them reflected the same sensibility. In America, they made this not a survival strategy, but an insight into the possibilities of a world that offered life as it should be, rather than as it actually was.

The trajectory of Massimo and Lella's professional careers is unusual. They were among the first to embrace the idea of design practice as a multinational business that could combine creativity and the trappings of corporate values. Unimark set a pattern for the handful of global giants that today combine branding, communications, advertising, and design, whose employees run into the thousands, and are owned by shareholders rather than designers. The Vignellis decided that this was not the approach for them. They went back to a more personal way of working and demonstrated its continuing relevance in the contemporary world. They demonstrated with remarkable eloquence how important it is for a creative designer to have a point of view. For them design is a matter of culture as much as it is one of problem solving. It is about how we live, more than how to entice and manipulate the consumer to consume.

Deyan Sudjic, *Director, Design Museum, London, England*
January 2014

Preface

I first met Massimo Vignelli in New York, at the Tenth Avenue office of Vignelli Associates, in 1987. Lella breezed through at one point, but we did not speak. As a sincere but naive graduate student focused on graphic design, I had begun researching Unimark International, a topic that was bigger and broader than I realized—one that might have been too intimidating if I had truly known what I was getting into. Yes, ignorance can be bliss. With more research and insight, what began as a graduate thesis eventually turned into a book. *Unimark International: The Design of Business and the Business of Design* was published by Lars Müller in 2010.

Massimo and I met, emailed, and phoned many times over the years. Sometimes Lella was pulled into our conversations, but she always seemed like a busy woman—briefly interrupting her tasks to jog Massimo's memory and clarify a point or two before walking away. Frankly, she was a bit intimidating, but finally I sat down with Lella, alone, and listened to her stories. I saw a new side of her: vivacious, talkative, dryly humorous, and definitely engaging. I am thankful for the many times we've seen each other since. I wish I had gotten closer to her sooner and talked with her more. Sometimes ignorance is simply ignorance.

As was true with Unimark, the Vignellis' story is illuminated through understanding cultural contexts and the flavors of changing times. So much of their work surrounds us now, so many of their ideas about visual form and communication have been embedded into contemporary American life, that it is hard to recognize how much the world has changed. At times, the Vignellis gave form to that world. At other times, they held resolutely to their own path as proponents of change challenged their thinking and railed against their form of problem-solving. Today, they articulate their position as vehemently as ever. Clients continue to knock at their door as they have for more than a half-century.

The world was distinctly different when modernism was rising, when they left Italy and first experienced the United States in the late 1950s. Massimo describes modernism as "the search for truth, the search for integrity, the search for cultural and intellectual enrichment." The Vignellis are modernists. They focus on design as a profession with the potential to make the world a better place—fighting ignorance; creating understanding; adding beauty, meaning, and elegance to the artifacts of everyday life. Their mission of "better design for a better world" has been consistent through a half-century of dedicated work. I believe in that mission, which is what inspired me to write this book and share their story.

With good humor and easy acceptance, Lella and Massimo have been gracious as I've asked questions and gathered information. I am humbled by their eloquence and inspired by the thoughtfulness that they, their family, friends, colleagues, and clients have shared with me. I hope that this story is useful as documentation of their creative lives. More importantly, I hope that it is an inspiration to others, particularly to students who are just waking in their passions and their potential to make a meaningful contribution to society.

Jan Conradi
January 2014

NOTE: *Much of the information in this book came from primary research. All direct quotes with the Vignelli family, unless otherwise noted, come from my interviews, personal conversations, or correspondence with that person.*

Acknowledgments

My life has been enriched by the articulate, intelligent, caring people who have surrounded me as this book evolved. It is difficult to thank individuals because it takes an amazing number of people to turn an idea into a book, and omissions are almost inevitable. In a blatant attempt at inclusiveness, I offer a grateful thank-you to all who shared information and provided support, critique, and encouragement while I was researching and writing this book.

I constantly urge my students to reach out to the designers who intrigue them. "It will change your lives," I tell them. Lella, Massimo, Luca, and Valentina Vignelli—you have certainly changed mine. I thank you for all that you have shared with me over the years, in hours at Massimo's table, on Luca's balcony, in Lella's office. I learned about feelings as well as facts on drives to downtown meetings, on a flight to celebrate the Unimark book in Chicago, around tables in Provence, over many dinners and drinks, through emails and phone calls. You've given me another book's worth of memories.

Family and friends learned more about my research than they ever wanted to know. Thank you for your patience with my enthusiasm. Don Kline pushed me to be better, edited my miserably rough drafts, challenged my assumptions, and clarified my thinking; I value your friendship even more than I appreciate your substantial efforts on my behalf. I am grateful to Charles Castilla for your assistance in touching up the many black and white photos for this book. Thank you to Dean Kaufman, for your beautiful photo of the Vignellis on the cover of this book. I can't look at that image without smiling.

It was enriching to be a participant in the RIT Master Designer Workshop in Provence in 2010, gathering information for this book and advancing my design skills under the watchful tutelage of Massimo, Lella, and Armando Milani. Thank you, Cynthia and Armando, for sharing your beautiful home with travelers who quickly bonded over design; that week is long past, but I'm glad that our conversations and friendship have continued.

I was fortunate to talk to many people who worked at Vignelli Associates, or Unimark, or both. Michael Donovan, from the earliest years of Vignelli Associates; Jonathan Wajskol, Rocco Piscatello, Michael Bierut, Graham Hanson, and Sharon Singer in the middle periods; Beatriz Cifuentes and Yoshiki Waterhouse in later times; and *many* others—your stories and assessments of the times, places, and relationships added personality to the facts. Vignelli clients and design professionals on both sides of the Atlantic, more than I can name, were consistently accessible and enlightening.

Some I must remember in the past tense. I am thankful for a magical summer afternoon in Beverly, Massachusetts, when Laura Hillyer shared wine and cheese and her purring cat, then dug in a closet to find her commemorative t-shirt from a long-ago birthday celebration for Massimo. On another beautiful day, Mildred Constantine (Connie) refused to let Massimo enter until he phoned birthday wishes to Valentina. He called, then we talked the day away. Connie and Laura were amazing women; I am glad my path briefly crossed theirs.

Thanks to the many people at Rochester Institute of Technology who aided my research in the treasure-trove of the Vignelli archives and who continue to make me feel that I have a "home" at the Vignelli Center for Design Studies and at RIT. Roger Remington was gracious about granting access to the archives and Katie Nix assisted me in finding things hidden in the mass of boxes. Nancy Ciolek and David Pankow are two more of RIT's best who encouraged me in their own quiet ways. Thanks to Ann Stevens for her final round of careful and thoughtful editing, and to Marnie Soom for design assistance. This book is enriched by A. Sue Weisler, who shared her wonderful documentary photos of the Vignelli Center. And, finally, special appreciation to Molly Q. Cort. This book in your hands shows Molly's wizardry at assembling a team and managing the book's production process. I am the author, but I couldn't have written this book without all of you.

Lella and Massimo Vignelli, c.1980

Our ethics demand the best from us,

in order for us to give the best in return.

Design is an encompassing profession,

not a job or a trade, but a profoundly

ethical profession that we should embrace

or reject. No room for the Philistines.

No room for vulgar minds.

—Massimo and Lella Vignelli

The Vignellis: An Introduction

Designers Lella and Massimo Vignelli have lived and worked in some of the world's greatest cities; traveled extensively and often; planned, designed, and focused on material goods for most of their lives; yet they are seemingly immune to the lure of consumerism. They have not succumbed to typical marketing attitudes that continually demand more, newer, different, better. In fact, they rail against a frivolous understanding of the first three and craft a cautious relationship with the fourth. Better, they ask? Why is it better? How much better? Better for whom? Better for what? Better for how long? From such questions, they craft meaningful answers in beautiful and functional forms.

Their work—publications, packaging, furniture, housewares, showrooms and architectural interiors, identity programs, transportation graphics, watches and jewelry, and more—has been well-documented. Although people may not recognize the Vignelli name, the Vignelli work is familiar because people use it: guides to America's National Parks and Fodor's Travel Guides; wayfinding systems for the subways of New York and Washington, D.C.; the trains of the Great North Eastern Railway in Britian. It is seen as exhibitions for museums as diverse as The Louvre, Corning Museum of Glass, and Minneapolis Society of Fine Arts; interior design and furnishings for Saint Peter's Church in Manhattan; and brightly colored Heller plastic dinnerware. It is diverse and international: identity and interiors for the World Trade Center in Amsterdam, International Design Center NY, Barney's, and Italian restaurant SD26; showrooms for Poltrona Frau; logos and packaging for Feudi di San Gregorio winery in Italy, and Bloomingdale's and Saks Fifth Avenue in New York.

While Vignelli work has informed and functioned as a part of the cultural landscape for decades, the tangible artifacts, interesting as they may be, are but snippets of a larger story. The Vignelli story of design is also a story of their lives and interactions, influences—and influence upon—many, many others in the United States, in Italy, and around the world.

Massimo is an extrovert. Gregarious, articulate, outspoken, he delights in working the crowd that is usually equally delighted to be in the room with him. Lella is more reserved, poised, privately determined but publicly quieter. She is less often directly in the spotlight; she seems to have less desire for it although she is no less deserving of its shine. She saw no benefit in competing for publicity, and often she was simply too busy acting as the force behind the scenes, helping to assure success for both of them.

Together the Vignellis have been confident and consistent in their choices and earnest in their vision. They have been focused on enhancing meaning and creating lasting work in a profession that is too often ephemeral. That they've been successful in doing so is acknowledged through receiving the first United States Presidential Award for Design Excellence (1985 for the National Park Service Unigrid publication system) and Italy's highest design honor: the Compasso d'Oro (1964 for melamine stacking dinnerware; and 1998 for the identity system and signage for Cosmit, the company that organizes the Salone Internazionale del Mobile di Milano). In addition to these, they have received numerous awards from professional organizations and honorary degrees from universities around the world.

The Architectural League of New York honored the Vignellis in 2011. The organization's website states, "Massimo and Lella Vignelli are awarded the 2011 President's Medal in recognition of a body of work so influential that it has shaped the very way we see the world, and so perfectly conceived and executed in its specifics that each encounter with a Vignelli object or book or sign or space is a moment of delight. The integrity and consistency of Massimo and Lella Vignelli's work, their commitment to the essential, the timeless, the rational, and the beautiful, inspires now and will continue to inspire long into the future."[1]

Lella and Massimo find no contradiction in simultaneous and seemingly opposing forces. They embrace change as emphatically as they celebrate timelessness. They have a tremendous respect for history while they live enthusiastically in the present and eagerly look to the future. Their approach is holistic, yet they never lose sight of details. Ambiguity is a key element in their thinking even while they shape their days with predictably structured routine. They turn clients into friends, and friends become their clients. They speak like proud parents of the young designers who have grown under their tutelage, yet they readily challenge anyone who makes choices they perceive as detrimental to the design profession and by extension, to society.

Their message was formed early in their careers and it has been repeated confidently ever since: be disciplined, be appropriate, be consistent. Known for saying "design is one," in some respects the Vignellis are also one. Their work and their lives are united and seamless; the same standards they utilize with clients are applied to themselves. The result is a confident foundation and a rare level of connectivity that has strengthened through the decades, but it would be a mistake to assume that the two are identical or that time hasn't tested them individually, as a couple, and as professional partners.

Introducing their work in the 2006 book *Lella and Massimo Vignelli: Design is One,* Massimo wrote, "Our basic working concept is that the discipline of design is ONE. If you can design one thing, you can design everything. Subjects change, materials change, processes change, but the methodology remains the same and a creative, investigative mind proceeds with thorough discipline through the necessary steps toward the relative solution of the given problems. I say relative because nothing is absolute. Everything follows your own interpretation of the reality, your own discipline, your own creative force. Time, exposure, focus, and determination are the fuel of creativity."[2]

Lella and Massimo attribute their work's distinctiveness to their Italian origins. "Italy is a country where hypocrisy and ambiguity are at home. It is positive ambiguity because it is a plurality of meanings, not contradictions or indecisiveness as it might be here," Massimo said. "It is not that we studied or searched for it, it is natural and it comes out when we work. Even perceiving the differences is built in—for instance, reflective versus absorbing surfaces: these come from being exposed to and observing glass. Once you've learned it, it becomes part of your perceptions, part of what the Germans call *gestalt.* We recognized that we could bring these values to our office."

At the same time, blending European and American ways was also a part of their working attitude. Massimo said, "European culture is based on refinement, not change for the sake of change which is typical of Americans. When we arrived here [in the United States] we were missionaries because we had something to overcome: a mentality which we perceived as not healthy. It was a byproduct of ignorance and we were not very tolerant of ignorance."

Like most young couples, Lella and Massimo sought independence, breaking away from their families to define themselves as individuals and as a couple. "You need to have the same sort of preferences and that has been good with us; we know each other very well and we balance," said Lella. "We are complementary. I am practical; Massimo is disorganized and less practical. There is cooperation. It is not a pencil with two hands; it is sharing the same intellectual platform. I work with the materials; for me that is where the design starts. Massimo will draw."

The Vignellis often interrupt each other, finishing one another's sentences or elaborating on a thought. The habit bothers them both and it is something they continue to work on, but habits of a lifetime are hard to break. On the plus side, it is a sign of their constant sharing of information. Their big ideas are developed together, fully understood by both partners. Looking at their career trajectory illuminates meaningful realities in design practice, in the *how* as much as the *what* of design creation. The Vignellis have accomplished much and have earned admiration, criticism, and occasional jealousies from other designers. The Vignellis have been where many designers would like to be. Though they have stumbled a few times, more often they have been dramatically and consistently successful.

Lella and Massimo have led rich lives, and they continue to be energized by planning for new adventures, solving new problems, and absorbing new ideas. They enjoy a creative, productive partnership that has been shaped by their individual upbringing, their unique trials and opportunities, their multicultural experiences, and by their relationships with diverse and interesting people. Other designers, students, and scholars can learn from them and about them through numerous films and television documentaries (most recently Kathy Brew and Roberto Guerra's *Design Is One: Lella & Massimo Vignelli,* which was premiered in 2012) and through the Vignelli Center for Design Studies, which opened on the campus at Rochester Institute of Technology (RIT) in 2010. Their archives are at the center, easily accessible to all students, scholars, and curious visitors.

At the dedication for the Vignelli Center, Richard Grefé, executive director of AIGA, the professional association for design, said, "The Vignelli Center for Design Studies will be instrumental in defining the role of design in society and commerce. It recognizes and celebrates the work of Massimo and Lella Vignelli, who are arguably the most influential designers of the past fifty years, for they have demonstrated that design can make the complex clear, can enliven both popular culture and the civic experience, and can delight the human spirit."[3]

This is their story.

Lella and Massimo arrive in the United States. Cambridge, Massachusetts, 1957.

Foundation: Growing Up in Italy

Elena "Lella" Valle was born on August 13, 1934, in Udine, Italy, as one of four siblings in a family of professional architects. Her family called her Lella, and Massimo also preferred the nickname. He said, "Elena sounded too old. Lella had a modernist ring to my ears and I liked it in conjunction with Massimo, so she was stuck with it."

Lella's father, Provino Valle, was a respected architect in Udine, a city about one hundred kilometers (sixty-two miles) northeast of Venice. The Valles were not wealthy, but they were rising successfully in class-conscious Italy and the parents defined clear expectations for the Valle children. Lella said, "When we were little my father was always encouraging us to draw. I was the youngest child. My parents had four children, three daughters and a son— and he for sure had to carry on the tradition and become an architect. When my brother was taken prisoner in Germany during World War II, my father decided that the next in line, my older sister, should take up architecture because 'you never know what will happen…'" [1]

Lella grew up in a lifestyle that was comfortable though sometimes restrictive; she recalled spending summers in the mountains envying local farm children who had greater freedom to play and explore unsupervised in the outdoors. Provino Valle's architecture office was in the family home and at about age twelve, Lella began helping her father. She learned by copying drawings and listening to conversations about construction details. For several years, her brother Gino and sister Nani also worked with their father in what became Studio Architetti Valle in Udine; after their father passed away in 1955, both siblings continued with respected architectural practices and Nani became a professor of architecture at the University of Venice. It was assumed that Lella would follow a similar path.

Massimo, born January 10, 1931 in Milan, Italy, had a less idyllic family life. His parents' marriage was strained, and it ended when he was seven years old, setting the family outside the mainstream of Italian Catholic life and creating some financial stress. Massimo's father was a businessman in the pharmaceutical industry. His mother worked part-time as a nanny and sold her knitting and crocheting. Throughout his childhood, Massimo was never quite settled—changing schools, spending time with one side of the family or the other, always hoping that his parents would reunite—a typical situation today, but not so common in 1930s Italy.

Those years were difficult, but looking back, he is grateful for some of the lessons and values that his family upheld even through tough times. "My mother was ambitious and I think she wanted to plant a picture of quality in my mind. God bless the education I got through my family," he said. "My aunt was a big influence, and my mother. They taught me to be respectful, to be neat, to put something away if I took it out, to talk and dress properly—not for others, but for myself. It was a fundamental attitude: not doing something for appearances, but doing it because it reflects who you actually are."

The World War II years were, of course, tumultuous in Italy. Massimo said, "I remember the day the war started in 1940. I went with my great-grandfather to the square and we heard Mussolini talk. I was a kid and I didn't understand. It was a sad day, although everyone thought (or hoped) that the war would be a short one." For Massimo, already unsettled by his parent's divorce, the war created additional upheaval and displacement. In 1941, he moved from Genoa, where he was living with his mother's side of the family, to school in Milan, staying with his father, aunt, and grandmother. That house was bombed, so the family had to move. In 1942, he was in boarding school in Salò, Italy; in 1943 he was in school in Passirano, near his father's business in Brescia. He was back in Milan with his father in 1944. He usually spent summers in Genoa with his mother.

In 1944, Massimo and his aunt were traveling to his grandmother's home in Milan, choosing to ride bicycles from Passirano to Milan because trains were often in danger of being bombed. They were on a small road, near a bridge that crossed over the *autostrada,* when a small British plane flew low overhead. The pilot apparently decided to use that bridge for target practice. He fired his machine gun, strafing the nearby roadway. The travelers were uncomfortably close to his target, so they jumped from the roadway and hid in the bushes. Massimo prayed for his life, prayed for war to be over. The plane flew off, leaving the bridge intact, and the sobered travelers crossed over it and continued into Milan.

Lella's family was also unable to insulate the children from ugly wartime realities. From an upper window, Lella and her sister saw Nazi soldiers chase and shoot a partisan in front of their home. When the soldiers saw they were being watched, one of them fired through the window. Fortunately, the girls had already ducked and run.

War caused financial problems for the Valle family. In 1924, Provino Valle designed la Terrazza a Mare (the Terrace of the Sea); it was an icon that attracted tourists to Lignano in the Friuli-Venezia Giulia region of north-eastern Italy. He also completed a series of city and land-use plans for the Lignano resort and continued to be an investor until Mussolini commandeered the development. The Valle family never forgot it. Years later, some thought the experience was reflected in Lella's management of Vignelli Associates. She was particularly careful in organizing finances and establishing billing rates and procedures, often castigating Massimo for not being sufficiently attentive to this. Robert Traboscia, a designer at Vignelli Associates (and Lella's nephew by marriage) said, "Frugality is a Valle trait. Lella controlled finances for the business. I think that her watchfulness goes back to losing fortune in the Mussolini days."[2]

Massimo was bright and eager to learn, but school wasn't always a good experience for him, especially in high school (liceo). His father first enrolled him in the scientific liceo, but Massimo wasn't interested and didn't succeed. Things were no better at the classic liceo. He preferred hanging around a local cabinet maker's shop, intrigued by the furniture that a friend's family had commissioned. "I was just watching, but it was the first time that I thought about furniture being made; it was when I discovered that things could be designed," said Massimo. Decades later, he can still clearly describe and sketch the proportions and structure of that furniture. That experience was illuminating to him from a design standpoint, and it also typified the way he would approach information and experiences throughout his life. Things that impressed him were never forgotten, seemingly becoming part of his psyche. What didn't engage him, what he didn't enjoy, would be ignored or pushed aside as quickly as possible.

Massimo was fifteen. His poor scholastic performance couldn't be ignored, and only one viable educational option remained, so in 1946, his father had no choice but to relent and send him to the artistic liceo. There his experience was much different: the failing student became a leader in his class. Massimo said, "It wasn't pleasant to be flunking, to be the worst. What a boost for my confidence to finally be doing well! My father died in that year, but at least he got a hint that I wasn't so bad after all."

As the war ended, Lella and Massimo each focused toward architecture as their profession. Massimo discovered *Domus* (the Italian design and architecture magazine created by Gio Ponti in 1928). "I was fascinated by *Domus*," said Massimo. "I was buying the magazine with my food allowance, then I'd eat at a friend's house; I knew his family didn't mind. I still have the *Domus* issues from those years. I knew all the names of the major architects, and I was curious to learn more. I was finally finding something to be passionate about."

After his father died, Massimo was living in Milan with his uncle, Erminio Vignelli. One of his cousins, Enrico, was studying architecture at the time and doing freelance drafting work for the Castiglioni brothers. When extra help was needed, Enrico brought Massimo to the office. "It was a mind-boggling experience when I learned that an architect could design everything from a spoon to a city! They were doing radios, flatware, buildings, homes, furniture, exhibitions—that is what I wanted to do. I found that all these things had a common discipline," said Massimo. He borrowed the phrase *"Dal cucchiaio alla città"* (From the spoon to the city) from a respected mentor, Italian architect Ernesto Nathan Rogers, who may have gotten the concept from Adolf Loos. Most people credit Massimo for it now (and the Internet is full of wild misattributions), but Rogers used it to describe the diversity in Milanese architectural and design practice that caught the teenager's attention. [3]

Massimo was fortunate to be in Italy as he discovered that breadth of design interests because the educational approach in Italy—and an economic necessity for inventiveness during and after World War II—assumed natural connections between all facets of design. Lella explained that Italian architectural education was comprehensive and diversified, unlike the American schools where studies were, and usually still are, much more specific. She said, "Architectural training for designers has been important in Italy for a long time, and especially for our generation. The education of architects in Italy is very broad in its scope, encompassing architectural construction, engineering, city planning, design, and even including stage design. We were exposed to all of these areas in school. For example, we were given courses in furniture design as one of our subjects, and courses in product design. Because of this, the field of 'architecture' became much broader and more diversified." [4]

In 1948, Massimo attended the Brera Artistic Liceo where he developed a passion for art history, especially for modern and contemporary history. The school library was good, stocked with *Domus, Casabella, Lo Stile,* and many foreign magazines and books. Massimo spent hours absorbing their contents. One of his teachers was Guido Ballo, a historian and critic who wrote for *Domus.* At that time, "Milan was established as the main center of both design studios and related publishing activities. In fact, the founding of *Domus* and *Casabella* signalled a new era in the history of modern Italian design… [These magazines] regularly reviewed new projects and materials, maintaining the highest standards for the profession and setting the tone for the resulting professional debates."[5]

Massimo took full advantage of access to these magazines. Their focus on modern architecture shaped his thinking as he carefully perused each issue, fascinated almost to the point of obsession by the featured architects. Massimo learned of Le Corbusier and of his organization, the International Congress of Modern Architecture (CIAM). When he saw the promotional poster for CIAM VII (1949) in Bergamo, Italy (designed by Max Huber, who would soon become an influential figure in his life), Massimo decided to go to the event. It was a bold move for a young man just finishing high school, but curiosity outweighed caution. Meeting many of his architectural heroes left him starstruck and determined to emulate their successes. It appears that the earnest young man made an impression on them as well, opening the door to friendships and lifelong connections.

In the fall of 1950, Massimo was living in Milan. He enrolled in the architecture program at Politecnico di Milano. Though already acquainted with many of the leading modern architects in Italy and well aware of others around the world, Massimo had a growing realization of the close relationships between them. Knowing one person often led to others who were equally interesting. He became more aware of graphic design at this time in part because he met Max Huber, the influential Swiss designer who came to Milan to work with Studio Boggeri and later became the creative director for the Italian publisher Einaudi.

"Heinz Waibl [a favorite classmate since high school] and I were together all the time; talking about design and working on graphics and posters. We knew about Max Huber's work and we wanted to meet him. When we did, he told us that he had to move, so I offered him a room and he moved in with me for awhile. Because he was living with me, it was like I had a private tutor for design and typography," said Massimo. Many graphic designers cite Swiss designers Josef Müller-Brockmann or Armin Hofmann as their influences for modernist design, but it was Huber who initiated Massimo's interest. "This was in the early fifties, so it was before the Swiss wave became known through *Die Neue Grafik* [a Swiss magazine launched in 1958]. I was not aware of Müller-Brockmann until after I was in the U.S.," said Massimo. "Huber was the starting point for me for grids and graphics, and Albe Steiner, and the work at Olivetti.

Meanwhile, Lella was also advancing her education. She was a good student: disciplined, intelligent, and organized. After completing high school, she would continue the Valle family tradition by enrolling in the School of Architecture at the University of Venice. Studying was important, but the pivotal moment of her life in those years happened outside the classroom, while she was still a high school student. Lella accompanied her father to an architectural conference on Lake Como in 1951. She and Massimo met at that conference.

Lella and Massimo Meet

"My mother did not want to go to the conference so my father said, 'you come.' So, I did," said Lella. "We first went to Milano, and in the morning we were to take a bus to the conference. We came out to the bus and there were also six boys coming from the Politecnico; they were asked to work at the conference. [That group of young architectural students included Michele Achilli, Guido Canella, Aldo Rossi, Giotto Stoppino, Heinz Waibl, and Massimo Vignelli. Every one of them would become a respected architect or designer.] I was the only girl, so they were all very attentive," she said, laughing at the memory. "At the conference, my father was busy and Massimo was coming over and talking to me… I liked what he was saying, what he was thinking about work. And I liked that he had traveled, had been all over Europe. He was interesting."

Following the conference, Lella stayed with a cousin in Milan for a few days and saw Massimo again, then she returned home to Udine. From that time, their relationship blossomed though Lella's family had doubts about it, to the point where Lella's mother was steaming open the letters that Massimo regularly sent to her daughter. There are multiple opinions about the family's reservations, although the attraction between a teenaged daughter and a college student from out of the region logically made her parents watchful.

Son Luca said, "Italy was a very class-driven society and her family didn't want Lella to go out with Massimo because he came from a split family. Massimo was a brilliant young designer, but this was out of his league." Daughter Valentina said, "They were not so impressed with his academic record." Lella's niece, Caterina Roiatti, said, "He wasn't accepted because he wasn't an architect. But he was smart—my grandmother was a strong and dominant matriarch, and when she needed help, Massimo would come to help her. They then became friends."[6]

Many relationships, personal and professional, would advance because of his engaging personality and of course, eventually their relationship was accepted. "I knew when I saw her that she was going to be my wife; I felt that I heard my father's voice telling me that she was the good one," Massimo said confidently. "Because of my aunt, I grew up with a strong education in moral attitude—what it meant to be moral, to be honest—so these things were in my mind. When I met Lella, I saw that these things could be materialized in a person. Lella was different from the girls I'd known."

Whatever the reasons for familial hesitation, Lella was also determined to overcome them. She was not afraid of challenging their set limits in a bit of rebellion; it is possible that their concern enhanced Massimo's appeal. Lella was well aware of his academic struggles and equally aware of his ambitions. She said, "My family was not happy at first, but I saw value in Massimo and I was going to help him. I wanted to show my family that they were wrong. Our marriage was—and has been—successful, in part because we were able to get away and to define ourselves independently."

Forging an independent path did not mean abandoning their families, but it meant that the couple established their own perspective and balance. They were able to define themselves rather than adopt expectations or limitations based upon their upbringing. They would build from that foundation in new ways.

Caterina Roiatti said, "My mother [Mariolina, Lella's eldest sister] helped Lella while she was in school in Venice. She lived with my mother for awhile, and then later Lella was helping me. Lella and my mother were similar: softer, less harsh than others in the family. They were a little lighter, willing to have a life—and happier, I think. I saw this; I worked for over a year at Vignelli Associates and I lived in their house. They would always make a nice dinner and prepare the table. The rest of the family would work day and night in lifetime competition, but Lella and Massimo also cared about pleasant dinners with friends, museum openings, a vacation, a summer house."[7]

After completing his freshman year in Milan, Massimo transferred to the University of Venice in 1952. It was a stronger architectual program, and of course it was closer to Lella. She graduated from high school in 1953 and began her coursework in Venice that fall. They were both learning from Ignazio Gardella, Giancarlo de Carlo, and Franco Albini, who became a mentor for Lella's final thesis project. Lella thrived in a rigorous program of research, development, presentation, and critique, and she enjoyed the full range of required coursework.

The young couple was part of an ever-larger group, finding people with the same affinities who became lifelong friends—networking, though the term wasn't used at that time. They also discovered an affinity for making good things happen. When they learned that Le Corbusier would be giving a lecture in Venice, Lella and Massimo were in the audience with a plan to meet him. After the lecture, Lella presented him with a yellow rose, and the two aspiring architects offered Le Corbusier a personal tour of the city. He accepted their offer and so they earned private time with another famous architect.

Connections to a growing list of architects and designers also provided freelance opportunities for Massimo. By this point, he knew every leading architect in Italy. Massimo had to work, but he was excited by what he was doing. "Architects didn't have big staffs, so when they got a major project, they would hire for that project. I worked for many of them, one or two weeks in one office, a couple months in another, maybe six months in another," he said. "This exposure leads to affinities—seeing different people, different tastes."

He worked for Giulio Minoletti, who was designing interiors on the S. S. *Andrea Doria*. In 1952, he worked for Giancarlo de Carlo. That architect's work and attitudes toward life, work, and society were influential and appealing to his young assistant because they were focused and deliberate. "He was a terrific architect with strong professional ethics. De Carlo was utopian—against man exploiting man. His work had meaning, and his general attitude toward life, toward society, toward commitments, was very important to me. It began to shape my political point of view. For him, everything meant something. You draw a line, it means something."

"There is a point, a passage in life, where you begin to understand what is happening and it shapes your mind. It was hell in northern Italy in the Fascist republic when the Fascists were united with the Nazis. The Resistance had nothing; they were hungry, they would be shot on sight. The Fascist army would come into Milan on the tram, covered in guns and knives and everyone would freeze, then they would tell you to *move*. The bombings; the houses of torture…" Massimo grew quiet as he remembered those years and the ethical dilemmas they raised. He said, "If you are Marxist, it is for life. It means that your frame of mind is set: that designing is for good, for bettering society," he said. "It doesn't mean that you become a Communist activist, but when I grew up it was not that far from the industrial revolution and the exploitation of workers and women. I became aware by reading Marx, Engels, all the Marxist writers. They didn't teach this in schools."

In school, Massimo and Lella were typical young adults, exploring a range of thinking, holding on to some ideas and evolving through others. However, Massimo was already beginning to be recognized as someone to watch. At age twenty-one, his plan for a music store interior was published in *Domus* 273 (1952). *Domus* was known for its international focus; each monthly issue featured in-depth articles on famous buildings such as Le Corbusier's church in Ronchamp or Oscar Niemeyer's civic buildings in Brasilia, as well as innovative product and furniture design and critiques of international art exhibitions. It was uncommon for a young student to earn recognition within the authoritative pages of that magazine. Massimo's plan featured flexible furnishings suitable for sales during the day or lectures and listening events in the evenings. This idea of adaptable use reappeared years later as Vignelli Associates developed retail and commercial spaces. In 1955, he was again published in the magazine. This time (*Domus* 306*),* it was three pages of photos and narrative explaining his plan for a small family home with a distinctive gable roof and a central patio.

Massimo directed a campus architectural publication at the University of Venice with fellow student Aldo Rossi. This position provided an opening to contact leading professionals, and he persuaded both Le Corbusier and Ernesto Rogers to contribute articles for publication. It also led to an opportunity that would come back to haunt him later. A delegation of student publication directors visited Russia in 1954. Massimo identified himself as a Communist at that time and he liked to travel, so he joined the group despite the fact that the Italian government did not condone travel to Russia. He said, "I was hoping that the Russians would help to change situations in countries which were constricted by capitalism… Communism seemed meaningful until the events in Hungary [in 1956]. That was traumatic. The Russians were tearing down a democratic country that had chosen a form of government that they didn't like. After Hungary, I did not want to be a member of the party any longer."

Thoughts about America were also conflicted. Lella's brother Gino visited the United States as a Fulbright scholar at Harvard in 1951, also traveling to Taliesin and Fallingwater to see Frank Lloyd Wright's work. Lella and Massimo knew that Gino had a good experience in the United States, but at that time they were reading about and railing against the excesses of capitalism. Still, they were curious about American innovation, a curiosity spurred in part by California publisher John Entenza's *Arts and Architecture* magazine. Massimo said, "*Arts and Architecture* was a banner of enlightened America: of Eames, Ellwood, Soriano and all the architects on the West Coast with a different kind of architecture than the Europeans. It was modern, open, joyous—we thought if they can do that kind of architecture, maybe America is not that bad."

In 1953, Paolo Venini offered Massimo a part-time position with Venini Glass in Venice. Massimo worked at Venini until 1957, designing lighting fixtures and learning to unite a hands-on craft tradition with contemporary industrial design. At first, he spent mornings at the furnace in Murano and afternoons at school. He continued to thrive in studio courses while struggling with other required coursework. Examinations in math and sciences did not go well despite Lella's encouragement and assistance. Eventually freelance graphic design work took over his afternoon hours too. Massimo needed the income to help support his mother, and these professional experiences were satisfying, making it easy to shift his energy toward fulfilling work and away from frustrating academics. He never finished his degree, although he was awarded an honorary doctorate in architecture from the University of Venice in 1994. Meanwhile, Lella continued successfully in school.

Expanding Horizons, Crossing Oceans

In 1957, Massimo was awarded a fellowship at Towle Silversmiths in Newburyport, Massachusetts. Lella also wanted to travel to the United States, and her brother helped her arrange a fellowship at the Massachusetts Institute of Technology (MIT) to continue her studies. Her family would not, however, condone her traveling as a single woman. That obstacle was quickly overcome. Elena "Lella" Valle and Massimo Vignelli were married on September 15, 1957. Paolo Venini stood proudly as a father figure for both of them. "My mother was afraid that I would run away if they did not let us marry," said Lella. Only a week later, they arrived in Massachusetts. "When we first came over to the United States in September of 1957, we were still on honeymoon. We've stayed that way for many years," said Massimo as he smiled at Lella. She smiled back, rolling her eyes.

While Massimo was working, Lella was studying. The architecture students at MIT were working on design proposals for an addition to the Boston Public Library in Copley Square. She was excited to work with them, but she found that the approach was very different than in Italy. "The school projects in Venice were more theoretical, more focused on architectural history than our work at MIT," she said. "The university in Italy was very free. The professors would only come in one day—or half a day—a week to see your work. Then you were on your own… MIT was like high school. You had to go to every lesson. Each day you had to bring in the assignment you had been given the day before. That was new to me." [8]

As they acclimated to life in the United States, the Vignellis continued to be intrigued by the discrepancy between popular culture, as Massimo was experiencing at Towle, and a contrasting refined vision promoted by faculty and lectures at MIT. They were convinced that there were two Americas. One was conservative and commercial. "I spent a year designing forks, knives, and spoons, but nothing ever happened because marketing research said all the college girls preferred traditional patterns," said Massimo. He designed sleek pitchers of frosted glass with silver handles and spouts, but again market research rejected the works as too novel (though they were later produced and sold successfully by Venini-Christofle in Italy). The Towle experience began a lifelong distaste of marketing research for both of them. That distaste would strengthen during their involvement with Unimark International, a design and marketing company that Massimo co-founded with partners in 1965.

They decided to see "the other America" before returning to Italy. They drove south, then west, passing through New Orleans, crossing the desert to California. They marveled at the variety and the chaos of American cities and the vastness and diversity of the American landscape. Returning on a northern route, they stopped in Chicago to visit a friend they had known from school in Venice. He introduced them to Jay Doblin, director

of the Institute of Design at Illinois Institute of Technology. Doblin hired
Massimo to teach at the Institute and introduced him to people at Container
Corporation, including Ralph Eckerstrom, vice president of advertising,
and Albert Kner, director of the Design Laboratory. This led to a part-time
position researching packaging forms and materials in the Design Lab under
Kner's leadership.

From 1958 to 1960, the Vignellis lived and worked in Chicago. Lella was
hired in the interiors department at the architectural and engineering firm,
Skidmore Owings & Merrill (SOM). She met with architect Bruce Graham
and was confused by his attitude when he offered her a job. "He said, 'The
only opening we have is in interiors.' He seemed a little embarrassed. But
for me there was no problem because in Italy, all the architects did furniture
and design. At that time most architects in the United States did not do
interior design."[9]

Lella worked at SOM for two years, designing interiors and furniture for
corporate and legal offices. "I was quickly put in a position to coordinate
some of the interiors and office projects with young designers, because I
did have more background and experience. I was happy because this was
something I was doing—something I earned—on my own. They treated me
very well. When we left Chicago, they were sorry to see me go, and I was
sorry to leave, but we were dependent on Massimo's cultural exchange visa,
and when it could not be extended, we had to go."

While in Chicago, Massimo and Lella became good friends with Ralph
Eckerstrom. His Container Corporation office was across the street from
Lella's workplace. Workdays typically ended with Massimo and Ralph
walking to meet Lella, then enjoying drinks and wide-ranging discussions
on design, business, culture, and the patterns and possibilities of the world
around them.

Those years cemented in them a love for Chicago, though after 1960 they
never lived in that city again. "We do love Chicago because of Bauhaus
connections, of traditions in printing and typography, of congenial people.
But it is more than that," said Massimo. "I will give you a name that describes
everything—Carl Sandberg. That is Chicago. The sense of the prairie, the
sense of magnitude that you find there. New York never, ever had anything
like it. New York is a peninsula and Manhattan is an island and it doesn't
belong to America—it is a continent by itself in a sense. That is why we are

comfortable in New York; it is very European in one sense and very American in another and so it feels comfortable for an ex-patriot. But when you are in Chicago, you *really* come to America. You come to the prairie, you come to great dimensions, vast horizons."

The Vignellis returned to Italy in August 1960 and opened their office in Milan. They worked collaboratively on product design and also assisted other architects by completing architectural plans and construction drawings. Massimo was designing posters and publication systems. Lella was graduated from the School of Architecture, University of Venice and became a registered architect in 1962, the same year their son, Luca, was born. Massimo was teaching color theory and basic design classes at Umanitaria vocational school in Milan and at the Istituto Statale d'Arte in Venice. They moved to a larger apartment (conveniently located a floor above Franco Albini's architecture office), and their professional circle continued to broaden. With growing confidence and proven successes, their design ambitions expanded too.

They had four productive years in Milan, facing ideas and issues that have remained consistent throughout their career. Some involved visual methodologies, as they defined an objective language of form and structure. Graphic elements—color, typography, image—had meaning and functioned on a proportional grid or aligned in geometric precision. Some involved relationships, as the most promising of Massimo's vocational students began working in the office and the Vignellis began learning how to be effective managers and mentors in the business of design. Lella and Massimo became a productive team, establishing a professional partnership that built upon their individual strengths.

In his work for Piccolo Teatro (1964) and Biblioteca Sansoni (1963), Massimo refined an approach to typographic structure that gave powerful clarity and logic to content. His work was grid-based, minimal; relying upon efficient use of space and economical use of form without the added imagery or decorative elements that were more typically used in design of that era. He celebrated typography by emphasizing it, but with deliberate restraint, often using a single typeface with perhaps one weight variation and only a couple sizes throughout the solution. He added geometry and precision to the pages by using heavy rules (lines) to divide the space. These rules would continue to be key organizational elements in much of his graphic design, appearing in guides for the National Park Service, graphics for the Institute of Architecture, and posters for the American Center in Paris, among others.

At the same time, Lella and Massimo defined their approach to three-dimensional form and space. They designed exhibitions for the city of Torino for Italy's centennial, and for Pirelli. They created a showroom for Olivetti, interiors for Rank Xerox, and furniture for Poltronova. Whether they were designing furniture, dinnerware, or interiors and exhibitions, functionality was their primary focus. Geometry was clearly apparent; much of the work on products and furniture felt like architecture in miniature. As with graphics projects, this work was logical, emphasizing clean shapes devoid of extraneous pattern or distracting fussiness. They were not interested in producing purely decorative objects, but the beauty in their work was inherent in the structure and proportion of each product and in contrasts of surfaces and materials.

Lella and Massimo were ambitious and confident, particularly since their stacking melamine dinnerware was awarded Italy's Compasso d'Oro Award for design excellence in 1964. The next step was to expand their business, to have stronger affect on society by solving larger problems for bigger clients. This was easy to imagine but not so simple to do. "Large clients prefer to work with other large firms," said Massimo. "We were very successful in Milan, but we kept bouncing our head against the ceiling. After awhile there was no more stimulation in being at the top. We were looking for a higher ceiling."

They were not unique in this desire. Massimo was teaching with Bob Noorda at the Umanitaria school in Milan and in Venice. Noorda was a designer with compatible vision and strong credentials. He also wanted to advance his graphic design business. Massimo said, "We'd leave Milan with a suitcase full of books and magazines to share with our students, driving fast to Venice and talking about plans. We were always together, congenial in work and in friendship so we knew that a merger would work well."

The three offered a good blend (Noorda's wife was also a designer, but she did not work in partnership with him). Bob, an ex-patriot from The Netherlands, was calm and cool in contrast to Massimo, whose hotter temperament could be volatile. Both were powerful designers. Lella was disciplined, managerial— and she was already learning that her excellent design skills were sometimes discounted as others relied on her organizational abilities; this would become a continuing source of frustration throughout her career.

With plans underway for uniting professionally with Noorda, the Vignellis took a vacation and flew back to Chicago in the fall of 1964. They called

Container Corporation, intending to meet with Ralph Eckerstrom, but they were informed that he was no longer an employee. Eckerstrom had recently been fired because of internal politics and changes in corporate direction. They called him at home, then met to hear his plans and show the work they'd created in Milan. This meeting would result in a new direction for many people as the idea for Unimark International was born. Rather than partnering only with Noorda, they all joined with a group of American designers and marketing specialists to create what would soon become the largest design firm in the world.

Joining with the Americans opened access to a vast country where they saw great need and where they confidently expected to make great improvements. Massimo imagined colloquial, informal, inconsistent, and archaic communications being replaced by harmonious systems where form and function were unified with elegant precision and stripped-down clarity. It never occurred to him that a culture of consumerism was rising; that some people preferred a cacophony of expression; or that advertising's seductive promises of glamor and impatient flirtations with style would pose a formidable threat to his refined vision—or that this threat would be continuing for the entirety of his career.

Massimo and his "Max 365" perpetual wall calendar, designed in 1973 and still being produced.

1965: Unimark International

Unimark International opened for business in January 1965 with six founding partners and offices in Chicago, Milan, and New York. Officially, the founders were Ralph Eckerstrom, Massimo Vignelli, Bob Noorda, Larry Klein, James Fogelman, plus Wally Gutches as business manager, but Jay Doblin was also involved from the beginning. His name remained off the public record in deference to his leadership position at the Institute of Design. Eckerstrom was president, the others, including Massimo, were vice presidents. Vignelli, Klein, and Fogelman held the additional titles of directors of design.[1]

The name Unimark said it all. "Uni" implies *united,* or *unified* in English. In Italian, it was *one.* "Mark" could imply *marketing* as some people wanted, or as Massimo preferred to think, in Italian, "marco" meant *making a mark.* Altogether Unimark was *one mark,* one way of doing things. The final blended name satisfied everyone, but that blend needed to carry throughout the company's approach and effort. It rarely did.

Through Unimark, Massimo anticipated an opportunity to "spread the gospel of functional design." The Vignelli modernist visual language would strongly influence the output of the new company, as would reliance upon the Helvetica typeface (which was just becoming widely available in the United States. Unimark's use of Helvetica, and Massimo's continuing use of it after Unimark, would contribute to what became a ubiquitous worldwide presence). Their drive would be objectivity—to develop a form, a message, from a structural point rather than from a subjective, emotional one, and to create consistency through a unified and comprehensive systemic approach to visual identity. These were not unique ideas, but they were relatively uncommon in the mid-century United States. At the same time, the company, or at least some members of it, also intended to advance contemporary ideas for marketing research and public relations.

Entrepreneur Robert Craig knew nearly all of the important players in the design profession from his leadership role with the International Design

Conference in Aspen, and he observed their reactions to Unimark's promotional efforts. He was also a part of Unimark in the early years of the company. "There was a certain amount of jealousy and discomfort with Unimark's approach," Craig said. "Unimark was far reaching, and with the vision of a truly international approach, it went against the grain of the so-called hot shots who were ingrown in talent and in connections."[2]

Almost unbelievably, through a combination of charisma, enthusiasm, persuasive credentials, and a bit of luck, the newly formed Unimark prevailed over established, respected designers to secure the contract for a worldwide identity system for Ford Motor Company as their first major client. The development of the Ford system illuminated another aspect of Massimo's thinking that would remain consistent for his entire career. Though some designers, Paul Rand in particular, had urged Ford to abandon the existing logo, Massimo took an alternative view and recommended that Ford retain it. "There is equity in that logo," he said, arguing that the best decision was simply cleaning it up and integrating it into an orderly system.

"Do not deny history," he said. "American culture is based on novelty, on difference; Europeans are not interested in new ways as much as they are interested in refining a concept which has existed through the centuries. It is a continuing *evolution,* not a *revolution.*" It was a stance that he would repeat with other clients in years to come. The argument for respecting history and avoiding obsolescence was effective in engaging with clients, who often had mixed feelings about giving up an existing symbol. Suggesting a clean-up rather than abandonment of the logo often built a bond with the client, making it easier to advance other changes toward an overall plan.

Over the next several years, Unimark played a significant role in redefining the identity for many of America's leading companies: Alcoa, American Airlines, JCPenney, Knoll, Memorex, Trans Union, and many more. They did the same around the world: Agip and Dreher Brewery in Italy; Truman Brewery and Jaguar in England; Horters Limited, Standard Bank, Huletts Sugar, and Mondi Valley Paper in South Africa.

Unimark's work was not confined to identity systems. They designed signage and mapping for transit systems in New York, São Paolo, Washington D.C., and Denver; and signage systems for several hospitals. They created innovative electronics for Panasonic, consumer products for Gillette, and medical devices for Parke Davis. The company developed exhibition design, packaging, interiors, land-use planning, and even a visual system for an Olympics hosting bid. They promoted furniture created by designers in the Milan office. Massimo—and often Lella—were intimately involved in many of these projects. In the heady early years, the company exploded in size, employing about two hundred people at its peak in 1971.

For a while, Unimark even produced a design journal, *Dot Zero,* which was financially underwritten by paper manufacturer, Finch Pruyn. Five issues of *Dot Zero* were published (1966–1967) before Finch Pruyn withdrew financial support, leading to the journal's demise. Herbert Bayer named the journal, Massimo designed it, and Mildred Constantine (architecture and design curator at MoMA) directed the editorial board. The list of contributing authors for the first issue included Arthur Drexler, Martin Krampen, Marshall McLuhan, Bruno Munari, and Bror Zachrisson; equally diverse and visionary contributors were published in subsequent issues.

Initially the Vignellis stayed in Milan. Massimo worked with Noorda and a staff of young designers (mostly former students). It seemed like a dream come true for most of them. Franco Gaffuri was a junior designer who had been working with Noorda prior to the merger. He said, "We were excited to be part of an important firm that was planning for large projects and prestigious clients. We knew we needed experience at an important studio to learn what to expect in business. Becoming part of Unimark helped us because Bob [Noorda] was a creative person, but he didn't pay much attention to vacation, or money, or those kinds of issues. All of this was formally resolved when Unimark began, so things got better for us."[3]

Things did not get better for Lella when Unimark formed. She was forbidden by company policy, which Massimo helped to write, from having an official position within Unimark International. She was understandably furious when Wally Gutches, the business manager, broke the news. Rules against spousal hires were common in businesses of the time, and couples are still often discouraged from working together in American offices. In her case, the policy was only partially applied, but there was still disparity: Lella's work was contractual while Massimo held a very public role as a founder and design director.

Lella had to be assertive, had to defy company policy if she wanted a creative role, but it was only because of Massimo's support that she could take part in design development at Unimark. She was not operating from a position of strength. He was actively involved in nearly all Unimark decisions, meeting with clients, traveling widely, and selecting and giving direction to projects in most of the offices.

The Vignellis Move to New York

The Unimark office in Milan was successful, as was Chicago's, but operations in New York did not run smoothly in the beginning. Persuading Massimo to take charge in New York was not difficult. The office was in the Seagram Building, designed by his idol, Mies van der Rohe. How could he refuse? The Vignellis became twentieth-century immigrants, arriving on the dock in New York with furniture, suitcases, and trunks, just like previous generations. They had a three-year-old son, Luca, and their daughter, Valentina, would be born not long after their arrival. They quickly settled in with the help of Mildred Constantine [Connie], who was curator at the Museum of Modern Art, and Massimo took control of the office. Constantine and the Vignellis were well-matched: ambitious, engaging, and stimulated by one another's company.

"Connie was fantastic; she knew everyone," said Lella. The Vignellis met Mildred Constantine during their Chicago years because she was friends with the design leaders at CCA. She had been a curator for architecture and design at MoMA since 1943, and she had also been involved with the International Design Conference in Aspen from its inception in 1949. "Aspen aided my work at MoMA and kept me in touch with the talent, ability, and vision of a whole group of young people," said Constantine. "Massimo was one of them. He was always outspoken, sure of himself. What attracted me to him was the possibility within him to powerfully contribute to the world in which we are living."[4]

Constantine maintained a close friendship with the Vignelli family until her death in 2008. "She helped us tremendously; she was our mentor [at Unimark]," Massimo said. "Connie helped Unimark get the subway projects, she was editor of *Dot Zero,* she introduced us to the New York design scene, she collected our early work for MoMA. We shared countless Thanksgivings and we never had a small talk in fifty years. It was an intellectual relationship. She never said one word too many—just the last one, all the time!" he said, laughing. Constantine watched as the company rose, then fell. "I thought Unimark was very important, but the basis of their formation was idealistic—too idealistic," she recalled in 2007. "Individual ego was driving them, more than the idea of unity." Constantine would continue to champion the Vignellis' work for the rest of her career.

Massimo viewed his role as Unimark's leading advocate for design while Eckerstrom focused on building contacts, seeking new clients, and promoting the company. Massimo was confronting the pressure from marketing and salespeople, or as he liked to call them, "the philistines talking about money in the temple of design." Despite internal conflicts, all Unimark leaders came together to present major proposals and introduce solutions. "Presentations were great theater," said Massimo. "Ralph [Eckerstrom] would give a strong introduction, then we'd have a fantastic strategy story with Jay [Doblin] covering research and planning on where the client was now; where we wanted them to be. We'd have very high-level realistic comps, not sketches."

Bill Freeman, a designer in the New York office, described development and preparation for one of those presentations. "Bob Noorda was in New York for a month or so as we worked on the transit project. Watching Bob and Massimo work—when they put down sketches, they worked very surely, not fooling around. They knew what they wanted." He explained, "I was supervising production for the New York subway project, gathering materials and making Photostat mockups of the new signage. It was assembled in a beautifully bound book box, about 28 by 28 inches. Massimo liked to stage things, so the box was in the middle of the table; nothing else was allowed on the table. We had signs to size in the box, even a big overhead sign like you see over the entrance stairs. That was about eight feet long, and we carefully folded it and put it in the box. It was an impressive presentation—quite dramatic when that box was opened."[5]

Theatrical performance was evident inside the company as well. Massimo's absolute belief in his own message sometimes manifested itself in unusual ways. Evan Eckerstrom (Ralph's sons, Evan and Steve, both worked at Unimark) said, "Massimo's office included an arrangement of black file cabinets, upon which was glued his Compasso d'Oro design award—kind of like having the actual Declaration of Independence in the office."[6] For a time, all Unimark employees were required to wear white lab coats. Massimo got that idea from Franco Albini. The crisply pressed coats were meant to convey a sense of discipline and give a sense of unity, an attitude, to counteract "the sloppy, sporty American approach," which was too subjective for him.

Responses to the lab coats were mixed. Freeman liked them. "We all wore them; they made you feel like a doctor or better still, a Mercedes Benz engineer," he said. Most others were less enthralled, and clients weren't sure what to think. "My first meeting with the Vignellis was at Unimark," said Alan Heller, president of Heller, Inc., a firm developing housewares at that time. "I walked into the 62nd Street office, saw the lab coats, and at first I thought I was in the wrong place: is this a doctor's office? It didn't intimidate me, but it was different."[7] Eventually some of the younger designers in the Chicago office led an open rebellion, and the uniforms disappeared.

Unimark sought designers who had experience or education that was aligned with modernist ways of thinking. In 1967, Simon Jennings arrived from London as a student intern. "I was a naive and nervous Limey in New York, but I did figure out the pay phone… Upon calling the Unimark office, I spoke to Bill Freeman and he encouraged me to drop by. He could see that I was pretty inexperienced, but he looked through my portfolio with interest, saying 'Massimo will like this.' In my degree course, I had been strait-jacketed into following Swiss design in black, white and red with three-column grids, all cool and logical, clean and crisp. Later, I had an appointment with Massimo. He said, 'You understand grids. You are hired.' I started the next day, making mechanicals [production layouts] of Knoll furniture brochures."[8] Jennings' relationship with Unimark continued after his internship; he later worked in the London office and also in Chicago, working with Eckerstrom on the Volvo account.

As Unimark prospered and grew, company leaders were constantly on the move between offices, traveling first class, staying at top hotels. They were working hard, and they were living their dream; sparing no expense while doing so. The heady energy of those early successful years was intoxicating and it bred complacency. They mostly ignored the problems that were brewing. Ted Peterson (who became a director after working in several of the Unimark offices) noted, "the designers often disagreed with how Bob Moldafsky [director of marketing] pre-determined the design direction and how he would present our work… But on the other hand, Unimark was so rigid on so many issues that aesthetics often wouldn't come into play. That's where the conflict comes in, because a client company's personality and character was ruled out in favor of this system."[9]

Criticism of Unimark's design approach arose from within, but even more of it emerged from the outside. Other designers watched the company grow and attract major clients. In 1968, *Print* published transcripts of a moderated discussion on order versus disorder in the public environment. One of the participants was graphic designer Milton Glaser. His comments targeted Unimark by implication, though not by name. Unimark was on an upward trajectory at that point, "cleaning up" the chaotic landscape—especially in the United States—and dramatically shifting the visual identity of several notable clients including the New York MTA (signage), American Airlines, and Knoll (all guided by Massimo). Certainly Glaser was aware of the visual attitude that Unimark's designers were implementing and loudly promoting. He was not a fan of their approach.

Glaser and Vignelli have known each other since the 1960s. Despite sometimes contrary opinions toward their same profession, they share great friendship and mutual respect even while they argue opposing viewpoints. Glaser questioned the modernist claim that refined design would improve people's lives. He said, "I tend to agree with the notion of chaos as one of the few interesting entities we have to deal with in our lives, and I dislike most of the design planning that I've experienced, which aims to deal with this chaos. I'm concerned about the imposition of a design program that would reduce the variety by unifying the environment. Will this uniformity *actually* make the city more livable?"[10] Massimo's opinion was yes, it would.

"It worries me that all the solutions I've seen for some reason seem to fall into the same category," Glaser said. "Every designer from Milan, Zurich, New York, and Los Angeles seems to be using flush left Helvetica—the same type forms are coming into play, the same design criteria, the same sense of scale. I don't think Helvetica is invisible, although many people feel otherwise. To me, it has a marked stylistic relationship to a kind of attitude that prevails in certain designers' work. I think the reason it's chosen is not because of its legibility, but because of this stylistic attitude, which may not be very durable; in ten years it may change."[11] Glaser was wrong about the durability of Helvetica; its continuing worldwide dominance in the designed environment led to a full-length documentary film, *Helvetica,* by Gary Hustwit in 2007. Massimo was a leading protagonist in the film.

When outsiders were critical of the Unimark approach, by extension they were critical of Massimo. In urging corporate America to clean up its visual identity, he relied heavily on Helvetica and grids and encouraged all the designers within Unimark to do the same. Whether client companies were producing furniture, cars, air travel; whether the result was a signage system, a magazine, a map, an exhibition, or a package, Helvetica was often there. As Michael Bierut (whose design career began at Vignelli Associates) humorously noted in the film *Helvetica,* this typographic selection dramatically altered the visual landscape. "I imagine there was a time when it just felt so good to take something that was old and dusty, and homemade and crappy-looking, and replace it with Helvetica. It must have felt like you were scraping the crud off of filthy old things and restoring them to shining beauty..." This happened, he said, "[w]hen you [went] to a corporate identity consultant, circa 1965 or '66..." That was exactly the beginning of Unimark International.

Lella and Unimark

The Vignellis' daughter, Valentina, was born in January 1966. Lella balanced the demands of caring for their two young children, and although officially relegated to a role as a "consultant," she was actively involved whenever Unimark had three-dimensional work. She and Massimo often collaborated during the initial stages of a project, then she directed production and implementation. Lella managed the development of the new office interior when Unimark moved from the Seagram Building to larger quarters on 62nd Street in 1966. It was a striking space, all in black and white with charcoal gray carpet and modular furnishings; even a gallery/showroom. All the offices, with the exception of Milan, then adopted this approach. By its design, a Unimark office promised newness, change, and focus for any client who entered the space; it framed their expectations.

Lella was involved at Unimark despite the "no spouses" directive, although it was enforced for others within the company. Massimo wanted her there. He needed her business skills and trusted her judgment, so she became an influential presence in the New York office. He said, "She knew everything, every day; it was an active relationship." Although Lella was busy with their two young children, she was determined to be professionally active.

Designer Michael Donovan began working at Unimark because a friend knew of an opening. "My friend said, 'Call Lella Vignelli; she is looking for a multi-disciplined designer.' I still remember walking into a black-and-white environment and meeting this beautiful woman with a heavy accent, gray cashmere sweater, and beautiful jewelry," Donovan said. "We hit it off, Massimo wandered in, and I got hired. I would say that about sixty to seventy percent of the work in that office was graphic design, and the other thirty or forty percent was environmental or exhibition. Lella ran that and she also ran the office, dealing with the personalities."[12]

Sometimes from workers, sometimes from clients, Lella confronted dismissive attitudes about women in general and assumptions about her role specifically. This made it difficult for her, and she resented it. Diminishing her professional stature frustrated her and sparked some problems for the company too, because Lella's assertiveness in fighting for involvement and recognition sometimes caused tension in the office. More often, the ambiguity about her status and her relationship to a project was simply confusing. Sometimes Unimark staff, particularly those who were based in other cities, really didn't know who had the final word as a project evolved: Lella or Massimo? It seemingly never occurred to Massimo that there was a contradiction between her "outsider" status and her "insider" involvement, or with her right to be involved when other couples were not allowed the same flexibility. To Massimo, she was his partner; it was that simple. The company deferred to Massimo's wishes.

Lella was a key designer for interiors and exhibitions for Unimark, and she consulted with Massimo on many other projects. She designed a large trade show display for Panasonic, a Knoll exhibition on Park Avenue, and office interiors for Gillette. Although Lella was designated as responsible for managing these projects, her presence was somewhat suspect to construction workers on project sites. Decades later, a mix of exasperation and bitterness was still apparent as she recalled those times. "They'd say, 'Oh sweetie, what are you doing, hanging around? We have questions, send your husband.' I was critical when their work was sloppy and they resented that," she said.

Gender discrimination in the workplace hasn't completely vanished, but in that era it was overt. It was harder for a woman to gain respect and cooperation simply because she was a woman. Lella was young, beautiful, internationally exotic. She exuded stylish elegance; she spoke with a strong accent. She resented having to fight to be respected for her knowledge, her creativity, and her capabilities. She resented assumptions about a woman's role in a professional office.

She said, "In our class at the University of Architecture in Venice, out of fifty-three people there were just three women. In Italy, few women of my generation and from earlier generations were professionals. Perhaps for this reason, as architects we were treated as equals to men—as professionals. That is my reading of the situation. Here [in the United States], there were more women in the work force, but they mostly held subordinate positions. Since so few women held professional jobs, men naturally assumed that in the workplace, the woman was the secretary." [13]

Michael Donovan worked closely with Lella, saw the reactions, and often intervened. "She is right in her remembrance—I saw a lot of 'raised eyebrows' when she was looking the other way. One of my jobs was to be the 'male representative' dealing with vendors. I often was the bearer of bad news— letting them know she wasn't happy. Sometimes she would send me to a site meeting just because she didn't want to deal with a contractor's or vendor's attitude toward a woman in charge; a woman who controlled whether they would get paid. She could be tough as nails and they were a little intimidated by her—but most admired her. She was a pioneer in many ways. Now it's commonplace for a woman to be the final arbiter. It was much less so, then." [14]

The frustration for Lella wasn't only an issue of limited expectations based upon gender; it was also discovering a cultural difference in the process of design execution. Donovan gained first-hand knowledge of this when he traveled to Italy in 1971. He said, "I think her demands for perfection made contractors uncomfortable. Massimo and Lella both had a problem with the quality of most vendors relative to the quality they were used to in Italy. That was true of everyone: printers, color separators, typesetters, builders, exhibit fabricators, etc. When I went to Italy the first time and visited the Unimark office in Milan, I was taken to a job site—this was a high-end jewelry store. Unimark had done the brand identity, packaging, and the store design. No drawings, no bids, no schedule—the contractor was working from a small paper model the client had approved. The work by these Italian craftsmen was beautiful, albeit behind schedule. Massimo could never understand why it was necessary to create detailed drawings, so that was my job. In Italy they just waved their hands and the vendors would execute, beautifully."

"Here [in the United States] it is different. In Italy, you are an architect. It doesn't matter if you are a woman." Lella said, "I fought for women's involvement at Unimark, and I continued to fight when we had our own office. At project meetings, Massimo would say 'Lella will be responsible,' but sometimes clients did not want that. They wanted him! I always liked working on projects for Knoll because I did have respect. Robert Cadwallader [president of Knoll], said he appreciated me so much, he didn't even realize that I was a woman." It was an awkward compliment, but a little recognition was better than none. The Vignellis created work for Knoll during their Unimark years and the company remained a Vignelli client after Unimark ended. Continuity was a sign of a positive and respectful relationship, and the Vignellis often worked with the same clients for many years.

Massimo at Unimark

Massimo was sometimes a source of turmoil in the company. Normally that was related to his passions for design or against marketing, but once it was for a uniquely different reason. Not long after arriving in New York, he applied for a green card, but his exploration of Communism and visit to Russia from over a decade earlier aroused suspicion. "It was the time of the Cold War… The Immigration Department and the FBI looked at my files and discovered that I lied on my application [about having been involved with Communism], therefore they wanted me to leave the country." Unimark's business manager, Wally Gutches, played a key role in aligning lawyers to fight Massimo's deportation. The fact that Valentina was born here prevented them from deporting me," said Massimo. He is light-hearted in telling the story now ("All is well, that ends well…," he says), but it was tense at the time, and the issue flared up again later, slowing his path to American citizenship. Lella became an American citizen in 1979. Massimo did not attain American citizenship until 2001.

Unimark had a noticeable range of strong personalities, but Massimo certainly stood out as a stereotype of the expressive, emotional Italian. Absolutely committed to his work, he did not hide his feelings. Whether he was happy or angry, everyone knew. Most of the designers were admittedly awestruck by him, but if their personality or approach to design didn't align well with his, there was tension. Inevitably, those people had a short tenure in the office. Even people who had a long relationship with him could find his intensity overwhelming at times. Heinz Waibl, who has known him since they were teenagers and classmates, said, "Massimo is so enthusiastic, but it is sometimes *too much.*" [15] From one Unimark office to the next (and continuing throughout the years of Vignelli Associates), the designers were keenly aware of his intensity. Hearing him exclaim, "That is *fantastic!*" was a highlight in a busy day. Hearing "It's all wrong," or "It's a disaster!" would lead to redoubled efforts and long hours.

Katherine McCoy and Grant Smith were designers in Unimark's Detroit office. McCoy said, "We were always made aware of Massimo's arrival to our office, and hustled around getting everything spiffed up for him. His visits were a very big deal."[16] Smith agreed, saying, "Massimo was the source of a lot of excitement—we loved it when he came in. He was the big hero; some referred to him as the 'Design God.'"[17] Peter Teubner was in the Chicago office mostly, and designers there were a little envious of the operational differences between their office, where design and marketing were theoretically blended (but in actuality they were usually jostling for supremacy), and the one in New York, where there was no doubt that design ruled. "New York *was* Massimo," Teubner said. "Massimo handled his place like a king. He had his own world and clients there."[18]

Bill Freeman was happy to be in New York. "Massimo's English was atrocious, but I remember the warmth and confidence and mischievous good humor that flowed with such easy grace and charm from the man." He said, "After my father, he was the most influential man in my life."[19] Also in New York, Joel Margulies held a contrasting view. He said that he was "occasionally called to task by Massimo because I didn't really do things Unimark's way. I left stuff on my desk overnight. I didn't wear my white lab coat. Some of the things that I learned at Unimark became part of what I did later on, but they were so narrow in the way they made decisions. . . Unimark was very ritualistic."[20]

Unimark: Turmoil and Trouble

Unimark was short-lived. The Vignellis' involvement in the company was even shorter. In many ways that destiny was visible from the start. One of Massimo's best and worst characteristics is that his incurable optimism for his own passions can blind him to other issues and ideas. "Ralph, Jay, me—none of us were profit-oriented. It was a mission!" he said. Unfortunately there was not sufficient agreement on exactly what that "mission" was. With an absolute focus on *design* and the tantalizing prospect of internationally important projects, Massimo discounted the others who believed in *marketing* with equal enthusiasm. The issue was never adequately resolved.

Unimark's strategy was to open offices in major client cities, which was simultaneously a smart idea and part of the company's downfall. At that time, in the mid-sixties, there was no computer, no fax, no FedEx; only the telephone. The American interstate highway system was still being built. "It was practically horse and buggy days, as far as communications," said Massimo. In theory, multiple offices allowed Unimark to better serve major clients, and the plan was to acquire other clients to help support each regional office. The reality was different: shuffling personnel between offices was expensive, and a major economic downturn in the early 1970s shrank prospects for new business.

Within Unimark, the client work was shifting from large-scale design systems and identity development toward packaging and labeling for consumable personal and office products. This was not what Massimo wanted. Lasting impact was his goal, and he had real success in creating it. A prime example is the design program that he developed for American Airlines in 1967. Ironically, Massimo contradicted his usual advice to clients—maintain the equity of your history—in developing that logo. Favoring a purely typographic (Helvetica) approach for the logo, he recommended abandoning the eagle, which had been a consistent symbol of the company's identity. The flight attendants led a revolt in support of their eagle, and in a rare defeat, Massimo capitulated—somewhat. He would not create a new eagle symbol, but he agreed to incorporate one designed by Henry Dreyfuss, who had long been a consultant for the airline. "In the end, it was not so bad," was Massimo's grudging acceptance of the will of the client. The American Airlines identity system was in use until 2013. It was a lesson in listening and he learned from it; most of his clients expressed appreciation for his skill in listening and his clarity in communicating with them.

Unimark's troubles were multiplying. Other design firms were beginning to offer similar strategic approaches, usually with fewer overhead expenses to manage and often with more effective implementation. Unimark tried to continue on the same path that had worked for the first five years, but the success rate in acquiring clients was falling. David Law saw the irony in the situation. "If you consider that imitation is one of the best forms of flattery, evidently a lot of people thought Unimark was doing okay stuff, because it started having quite an influence," he said. "In fact, many of Unimark's competitors were former Unimark employees."[21]

The Vignellis were increasingly critical of Unimark's direction, but Massimo was unable to change it and Lella did not have an official voice in operations. Jan von Holstein was managing the London office and he analyzed the situation from there. "The conflicts grew as the finances eroded, and Massimo especially felt alienated by the business drivers in the company, for whom he never had much respect," said von Holstein.[22]

As president, Eckerstrom was conflicted and contradictory, intellectually aligning with Massimo, but acting in opposition as he emphasized public relations *for* Unimark more than consistency *within* Unimark. Others in the company focused on sales or research. Not everyone shared international motivations, no one was effectively managing finances, and certainly there was a lack of coordination with the overall management of the company so divided. Eckerstrom was not controlling spending. Massimo criticized him for it. "We would sweat here to send money to the common pot in Chicago. I said, 'Ralph, you don't have a pot, you have a colander.' Ralph's response was, 'You have to understand the American way.'"

The Vignellis were disillusioned. "Selling design services, designing things that did not make any sense… Design is not a fad, it is a business!" Massimo grumbled. "We are not involved in *persuasion,* we are involved with *information.*" He looked enviously at Bob Noorda. Being in Milan put Noorda far away from the Chicago headquarters, and for the most part, the Milan office was financially independent. "His good reputation was intact, and when the company disintegrated, he kept going with the Unimark name long after the whole thing ended in the U.S.," said Massimo.

From Chicago, designer Harri Boller noted that Unimark created some of its own problems by failing to follow through on contracted work. "Implementation was a problem for Unimark. Massimo was the best one for getting his work implemented; he had a strong personality and he stayed in touch with the client. In the Chicago office, it was more like you build up these great expectations, you make a great presentation, and then you kind of walk away from it. Massimo used a good phrase: 'seduced and abandoned,' and another that we used internally: 'Promising gold and delivering brass.'" [23]

"We would design beautiful work but we were not delivering," said Massimo. "We'd make great presentations, but something would get lost, it would begin to fizzle during the implementation phase. Lippincott and Margulies [a competitor, whether Unimark admitted it or not] was doing great corporate identities. Not only that, they were very, very good at implementing. If they did a bank, for example, you would go to that bank and you would see everything complete down to the last form. Unimark would do a bank, but it would never be completed and delivered."

Jay Doblin and Massimo were respectful of each other, but very different in their approach to work. "Jay was great at making accounts last forever," said

Massimo. "I'd go the other way, making a synthesis to a simple solution, and I would present only one solution. He would develop a huge strategy and drag out research and want to get marketing more involved in testing. He wanted *process* and he wouldn't deliver. I was interested in *results;* I wanted to deliver and move on to other projects."

Doblin also believed in obsolescence, which theoretically meant keeping a client for life as new product versions and updates were always needed. Vignelli adamantly disagreed and since that time has often lectured that "planned obsolescence is a crime." However, others were critical of Massimo, saying that he "had a good sense for glamorous projects, but not for money-making." He ignored the fundamental management cliché, "time is money" by rejecting designers' solutions that in his eyes fell short of the "greater principles" of Unimark. Both Doblin and Vignelli were obsessed with perfection and in that obsession, both contributed to the company's downfall. Unimark collapsed upon itself, with internal trials as much as outside forces causing the downfall.

Six years after helping found the company, the Vignellis left Unimark. They met privately with Eckerstrom to break the news. Massimo said, "I was physically tired from the whole thing, but the notion of hurting Ralph was very unpleasant to me." Though Lella was urging and supportive of change, it was not easy for her either. She said, "Now what? Here we are, family and all, not in our own country; what will it mean?" Hard as it was to break away, they were aligned in thinking this was a good decision.

Perhaps what Massimo interpreted as Lella's insecurity was her voice of cautious reason. "Every time I made a change, Lella was crying," he said. She defended her stance: "We were new in New York, with a young family, and it was not that easy—he thought he knew everything that was going on, but he did not," she said. After all, in their relationship she was the manager, the bill payer, and the more active parent. She chose this complicated role, and she was good at it, but each change meant additional worries for her until their lives and business were settled again.

Massimo, Lella, Luca, and Valentina. At home, 1974.

1971: The Rise of Vignelli Associates

In April 1971, Massimo resigned from Unimark, in part because the Vignellis wanted to work openly in partnership. Bill Freeman said, "Massimo and Lella were the driving creative force behind everything that happened in the office. When he left, it was like turning off a light bulb." Though it was detrimental to the already-struggling Unimark, this decision was a good one for them. Their public and private lives were more fully reconciled in a surge of new energy.

They chose to stay in New York, establishing Vignelli Associates from their home in Riverdale. They were happy to operate officially as partners, and their experiences with Unimark framed their thinking about business. "No middle managers, no focus groups!" said Massimo. "Not so commercial!" said Lella. Design projects that weren't viable at Unimark because they were too small to generate sufficient income—books and furniture, for example—were embraced by the Vignellis because they offered opportunities to develop high-quality design for products with longevity. Being small after being part of something so big created a new focus in the office, especially at the beginning when Michael Donovan was the only employee. Donovan stayed at Unimark for a few months to complete some unfinished projects, then he rejoined the Vignellis.

Massimo said, "After Unimark, our office felt quiet, and that was welcome. Our real nature returned and we had an office that worked. As much as we were doing things together before, because Lella was always a supporting column for Unimark, it was natural for us to work as Vignelli Associates. We quickly got more work, more interesting three-dimensional work." Personality played an important role. Industrial designer Niels Diffrient said, "Two words describe the Vignellis: style and charm. They use both as needed. But you also get the consistency—the same high design quality… The Vignellis, combining their sense of style with their charm, have broken through." [1]

Donovan has fond memories of those days. "Vignelli Associates? 'The Associates' was just me, at first. Being in Riverdale was about as intimate an experience as one could want. I was living in the Village and driving up to Riverdale every day, so one of my chores was to make messenger runs. I was the only designer. I was cooking, babysitting; I really was part of the family. Sometime in those months, they bought a dog, a gray Weimaraner [Massimo called it "a Bauhaus dog"]. I would be working and Valentina would come down and hang out with me. She would sit on my lap while I tried to work, and the dog was there beside us. When they would go to Italy, I would just move in so that I didn't have to go back and forth."[2]

It was an idyllic time. The studio was on the ground floor of their townhouse in Riverdale. The designers worked at large tables, enjoying a view over the Hudson River; classical music playing on the radio in the background. (They remembered Karl Haas' show: *Adventures in Good Music* as a favorite part of the morning.) Around one o'clock, everyone would stop for lunch, usually with Michael and Lella cooking together. The days passed smoothly, with little separation between creative, business, and personal life. Clients became friends, friends were clients, and they entertained lots of visitors from Italy and elsewhere; the spare room was rarely empty. There were beautiful sunsets and there were parties. Family and friends filled the dining room, gathering at a long green marble table surrounded by Mies van der Rohe's Brno chairs.

Donovan often helped prepare for parties. "I would work late, and it just kind of flowed: work, lunch, work, cook," he said. Lella did not like having a lot of people in the kitchen, but people tended to congregate there. "She would say, 'Get out of the kitchen! Get out of the kitchen!' and chase everyone out, and we'd be in there cooking and drinking wine. The menu was always pasta, but never exactly the same—there was always some new little twist; things like pasta with artichokes, which Massimo loved, but I had never had before."

Luca and Valentina were in school most of the day, but when they returned home, they would stop by the studio. Luca said, "Massimo was always excited by new designs, excited that they would be produced, and he was generous at showing things and sharing ideas with us. I think he really did want to know whether I liked something or thought it was interesting. I remember when they were designing the Heller stacking cups. I was about eight. They had a prototype and they said, 'put your hand in it, let me see how it fits in a child's hand. Does it feel comfortable?'"

"When I was younger still, they were doing design for American Airlines," said Luca. "That logo went on everything: planes, trucks… They designed for Knoll, and that truck had the name on the side. These things were around the office as presentation models, so I had plenty of cars and trucks to play with. It was a lot of fun. I remember getting the big model that they used for presenting the American Airlines plane, which unfortunately I destroyed over time."

Now that he was more relaxed, Massimo's innate playfulness and power of creative observation became even more apparent. He could seemingly find inspiration in anything. During the Unimark years, Massimo designed a new graphics program for Knoll International, and in 1972, the Vignellis were asked to plan a Knoll exhibition. It would be installed at the Louvre in Paris, then it would travel to other locations, so portability and ease of assembly were important. One of the challenges of this exhibit was creating focus on the furniture because the space in the Louvre was cavernous, with forty-five-foot ceilings.

"Lella and I were working on the project, looking at the floor plan and looking for inspiration," said Massimo. "Behind me, on a shelf, were some of those plastic cubes from Canal Street. At one point I grabbed them and tossed them over the plan, saying this is it! We will use cubes." Lella suggested that the cubes should be on casters so that they could be placed in the best way in any space. The eight-foot cubes created a logically scaled space relationship for displaying the chairs. Some cubes were transparent on all sides, some were enclosed except for the front and back. Some were doubled in a stack, allowing an audiovisual display to hover above. As usual, Lella managed the production for the project.

"The Vignellis have long excelled at exhibit design…," wrote Martin Filler in *Progressive Architecture.* "Making the space serve the objects becomes the first charge of such an assignment. This was the case at the Louvre in 1972, when the quintessentially modern furniture designs of Knoll International were exhibited in a setting more usually hung with vast canvases set in gilded frames. The Vignellis' dramatic displays—Plexiglass vitrines bathed in downspots amidst deep, dark backgrounds created a sensation,"[3] The cube concept of adaptable display spaces to organize a more intimate sense of scale surfaced again in 1979, evolving into flexible, modular interiors for the J. Magnin retail store in Los Angeles.

There was a tremendous amount of work being done at that time, including identities for Bloomingdale's and Saks; signage projects; a dormitory for Williams College that required interiors, furniture, and architectural signs; and new housewares products for Heller. Donovan was working primarily on three-dimensional projects with Lella; sometimes assisting Massimo with production for graphics projects. Design production was a manual process in those days, and the volume of work meant that more help was needed. Within a year, they needed more room.

Just when they began seriously looking for new office space, Bob Moldafsky called from Unimark's Chicago headquarters. His news was both exciting and sad. Unimark's financial and managerial difficulties were mounting, so the company was closing its New York office. Moldafsky asked if they were interested in taking over the space on 62nd Street. Yes, they were interested. The lease was transferred, and in 1972, the Vignellis went back to the office they'd designed for Unimark.

Expanding the Office: Return to 62nd Street

Part of the Unimark space was temporarily sublet to another tenant, so Vignelli Associates moved into what had been Unimark's big conference room. However, Massimo's office was exactly as he'd left it. "All things considered, it was a very generous offer. We were happy about it. It hadn't changed at all: my table was there, and the Brno chairs…," he said. They simply switched the name on the door. They hired a graphic design production assistant and a secretary. Shortly after, the sublease was ended and Vignelli Associates expanded to take over all of the original Unimark space. The office stayed on 62nd Street until they moved to Tenth Avenue in 1985.

By this time, there were actually two Vignelli companies, which reflected the variations and range of projects they were doing. Vignelli Associates was the larger company, focused on graphics, corporate identity, publishing, and environmental and interior design. Typical of most design firms, it operated on fees for services. The other company was Vignelli Design, which focused on developing products: predominantly housewares, furniture, and jewelry; compensation was based upon royalties. While it made sense to create these two business entities, doing so added extra work in record-keeping and financial management. That was Lella's responsibility.

Protecting Lella's creative time became increasingly difficult as the company grew. In 1975, they found a perfect solution, asking Paolo Venini's daughter, Laura Venini Hillyer, to become the office manager for Vignelli Associates. Hillyer was living in the United States, widowed with grown children, and she was excited to have a new professional focus. Lella helped her resettle in New York and she quickly became as much family as employee. She kept a watchful eye on Luca and Valentina, who joked that she was their "spare mother." Hillyer kept an eye on everyone at Vignelli Associates until she retired in 1992. "When you are new someplace, your survival can depend on finding someone close to authority to ask important questions. That was Laura," said designer Michael Bierut. "She was on the front lines of making the business function." [4]

Hillyer managed most administrative tasks: accounting, writing proposals and contracts; she assisted Lella in keeping everyone on task. "Seeing the office go from five people to so many—those were very creative years, combining great excitement and a lot of hard work," said Hillyer. The busy routine was predictable. She said, "I usually left the office about 5:30, but they often stayed and worked until after 7:00. Lella was working on products with David Law. Massimo was the genius in graphics. It was a tight circle with those three." [5]

As Massimo's personal assistant, Hillyer kept track of his hours, stayed in touch with his clients, and actively guarded his time. "Peter Eisenman [American architect and friend of the Vignellis] called me 'The Wall of Jericho,'" she said. Though Massimo was her focus, he was not "the boss." "For business decisions, I always went to Lella; I didn't even bother Massimo," she said. Hillyer did, however, coordinate the occasional search for his lost pencil, sounding an alert over the intercom that had everyone retracing his steps through the office until the favorite tool was found. His accuracy with that pencil was legendary.

"It was exciting to watch him work," said Luca. "He has an amazing facility in drawing, so as a kid of any age—even now—it is great to sit by him and see how clear and to the point he is in designing, whether it be a letter in typography or an object—a chair, or a bottle. He wouldn't make rough sketches to get to a final; he would go straight to the final in one step. If it was a question of a range of possibilities, he might draw ten or twenty options— but they were all finals. It was never correcting or erasing a line or fixing something. That kind of magic impresses the clients but it wasn't calculated to impress, it was just a natural outpouring."

"Lella was the spine of the whole place, not only working on design but supervising the production, going to see the clients," said Hillyer. "If Lella was not happy, we could tell from her footsteps. The secretary and I would hear her coming and think, 'God forbid, what did we do?'" Family, employees, clients, and suppliers are consistent in describing Lella. She was "the center," "the rock," "the foundation" of Vignelli Associates. Luca Vignelli said, "She was the one to think things through to many different levels: is this design feasible; does it have a basis in reality; is it practical; can it come in on budget for the client?"

The Vignellis believed that design was a relevant tool to make the world a better place. They consistently advocated for the power of design by their actions, in their own work, through interviews and public statements, through writing articles, and sometimes through consultation. Massimo and Lella were involved in diverse projects for the public good, including such varied projects as New York subway signage and maps, studies of Fifty-third Street furnishings and lighting during the Unimark years, and supporting AIGA educational and non-profit initiatives in the 1970s and '80s.

In 1974, the U.S. Department of Transportation asked AIGA for guidance in designing a set of symbols for use in signs at transportation facilities and other public spaces. AIGA selected a committee of five men—Seymour Chwast, Thomas Geismar, Rudolph de Harak, John Lees, Massimo Vignelli—to study existing, usually site-specific symbols, and create recommendations for this project. In 1979, designer Lanny Sommese wrote about the importance of this work in the journal *Novum Gebrauchs Graphik*. "While McLuhan's 'Global Village' becomes a reality and jumbo jets whiz international commuters traveling from one culture to another, the need for symbol signs which are consistent, clear, simple to comprehend and surmount the language barrier is paramount."[6]

The committee analyzed twenty-four symbol systems from around the world, then Roger Cook and Don Shanosky were commissioned to develop a set of thirty-four symbols based upon the committee's recommendations. These were initially tested at Dulles (Washington, D.C.) and Logan (Boston) airports, and implemented in Boston and Philadelphia for the 1976 American Bicentennial celebrations. In 1979, sixteen additional symbols were added; the set is in the public domain (and is available for download through AIGA and other sites). The Society for Environmental and Graphic Design (SEGD) and

Edward Boatman's *The Noun Project* still encourage widespread use of such symbols as an effective and efficient alternative to costly multilingual signs.

In 1977, AIGA sponsored a national seminar, Communications for Nonprofit Institutions. Subsequently, with the help of a grant from the National Endowment for the Arts, AIGA published *Graphic Design for Nonprofit Organizations*. Massimo provided the concept and design direction for the book. It was divided into two parts: Guidelines, explaining the components of design; and Prototypes, illustrating how two different non-profit organizations could use the design components to build clarity and cohesiveness in their message. "The main purpose of this manual is not to generate sameness or fads, but to provide tools to develop individual programs to fit individual situations," wrote Massimo. "It is also intended to support the efforts of designers dealing with management—to illustrate the necessity of investing in a coordinated graphic design program." Though some aspects of this book are now technologically outdated, the rationale and explanations are still clear, and sadly, many non-profit organizations still lack effective, unified communication programs.

The Vignellis were constantly busy with an ever-widening clientele and they were solidifying their reputations for high-quality work that was grounded in practicality. They treated clients with respect and approached each project with a sense of excitement. In years to come, the words "elegant, refined, and timeless" were often used to describe their work, but perhaps more meaningful words were "consistent and powerful."

An immense design project that clearly showcased the Vignellis' abilities began in 1977, with the interior of Saint Peter's Church on Lexington Avenue in New York City. It was a challenge because they had to create a sanctuary that functioned for both liturgical and secular uses—for religious ceremony as well as for concerts, theater, lectures, and conferences. From the beginning, they found a kindred spirit in Pastor Jared Stahler. Stahler said, "Massimo once told me that one of his life goals, one of his passions, was to rid the church of rubbish. I knew instantaneously that we would get along. Of course, his primary concern was design rubbish and my primary concern was theological rubbish. Two different disciplines, to be sure. But one focus."[7]

Lella said, "They wanted to use the space for so many things, so from the beginning we asked, 'Is this a church?' We said it needed another name and the question was, what do we call it? We said it is a 'moral space,' so that is how it was described." They developed a total design concept emphasizing granite and red oak throughout the interior. "These are noble materials—thick, solid, and long-lasting," said Lella. Like the Knoll Louvre exhibit a few years earlier, modular components were key to functionality in the space. The pews look permanent, but hidden castors allow pews and platforms to be endlessly rearranged. The kneeler flips down from the back of the pew when needed. Simply lifting up its top to expose a cushion turns what was a riser into comfortable seating.

Lella said, "We've designed many tables, but when we thought about designing God's Table, we knew it had to be large and impressive." Massimo flew to Germany to research the organ pipes; Lella specified lighting. They thought about the rituals of the liturgy and planned for them; they created ceremonial objects in polished silver, then designed convenient and secure storage spaces for them. They thought about the shape of the priest's alb (robe), designing a chair with the seat disconnected from the back so that the alb could drape through rather than be wrinkled by sitting on it. They thought about the significance of marking the transition of the space from secular to spiritual use, designing a simple processional cross. Stahler said, "The sanctuary is marked as a church when the cross is placed in its stand. There is no missing this simple, but profound, act."[8]

David Revere McFadden, curator of decorative arts at the Cooper-Hewitt Museum, New York, reviewed the final results. He wrote, "Interior design has long been a core activity for the Vignellis, bringing together Lella's European architectural training and her unique perception of form and color with Massimo's disciplined and ordered spatial sensibility, based on surface texture, light, and refined proportions. Their work is highlighted by exceptional commissions, including the interior and furnishings of Saint Peter's Church in Manhattan, a project that revealed the rational poetry of the Vignellis' approach to a highly charged symbolic space."[9]

Everyone in the Vignelli office was invigorated by constant new creative challenges and they worked with great dedication through sometimes long hours. The Vignellis did not compromise on the caliber of their solutions when the schedule was overflowing and the atmosphere was intensely charged. Donovan said, "The office had a great spirit and Lella could be a lot of fun. Everyone had absolute confidence—especially the women—that if they found themselves on shaky ground, she would calm them down. We could go to her and get good advice. She kept people's spirits up, but she was tough too. She was the one who gave the bad news, but fortunately I never had any bad news. It was very clear that she was in charge. The clients knew it too. She was the person that everyone had to satisfy, no question about it!"[10]

"Lella pushed everyone hard. She pushed Massimo hard," said Donovan. "There were spirited discussions between them around virtually everything because Lella was always more pragmatic. She understood that at the end of the day you had to get it built. She understood things like drafts and angles; when you mold something you have to be able to get it out of the mold. Massimo would want to make a shape absolutely one hundred percent razor straight and Lella would say, 'No, no Massimo—it's got to be two degrees so it can come out of the mold!' I would hear 'Massimo! You are so stupid!' but he would just ignore her. I was in the middle; it was like being a ping pong ball."

Designer Yoshimi Kono said, "They were often yelling at each other, but that was just the way they worked. I could see Massimo's point of view, and I could see Lella's clear understanding of the client side too. It was the combination that made the Vignellis special."[11] Designer Sharon Singer, who worked primarily with Lella in the interiors area, agreed with Kono. She said, "Massimo got to do a lot of the design, especially the two-dimensional work, but Lella always had input. She helped to keep him in line. For other projects, she had definite ideas and then Massimo would help edit. Their vision was very much attuned."[12]

Lev Zeitlin worked on model-making, three-dimensional projects, and anything else that Lella needed. He too had first-hand experience with their debates over production issues. "It was an in-house joke that we invented 'Massimo terms' like 'magic joints.' We would tell him that there was a problem and he would say, 'What do you mean, it's not going to work? It's so easy!'" said Zeitlin.[13] Because the Vignellis surrounded themselves with a team of smart and effective people, most things did seem easy. Massimo's meticulous drawings and Lella's crisp descriptions were passed to others for development and implementation in a creative process that flowed smoothly most of the time. There was genuine pride in a job well done at every stage of that process.

Massimo said, "From the beginning of Vignelli Associates, Lella was supervising and controlling the situation, and she always had assistants to help her—that kind of help was fundamental. We never argued about that role, I knew it was taken care of and so did Lella, and I always appreciated her contribution on that side of the business and family."

The initial stage of a problem, establishing the direction for the work, was what Massimo relished, so he often took the lead (and he did so exclusively for graphic design, since it was not Lella's area of interest or expertise), but they constantly consulted each other. "She was correcting, pointing out reasons for change, etc. If her point was not convincing enough for me, I would do it my way, but that was rarely the case." It became her task to shepherd the work through the remainder of the development and execution phases.

Although Lella and Massimo understood their joint decision-making, others did not always recognize the equality of their partnership. In early days, even if work was a collaborative effort, many publications edited the credits, citing Massimo only. Lella was justifiably angry about this; angry at Massimo and angry at the writers. "I'd go to the office in the morning and check the mail," said Massimo. "Any magazine that would show just my name [as designer], I'd make it disappear." Their professional credentials were more accurately acknowledged over time and now they laugh at those memories. Massimo said their partnership truly began after the Unimark days. "We grew together and our discoveries came through the exchange that happens when you are working closely. Lella had to fight for recognition for her achievements."

Both of them could be loud when they were angry. ("When we argue, we revert to Italian," Lella said.) They were stubbornly insistent when they felt they weren't being heard, but the drama always blew over, and the engaging personalities of both Vignellis quickly returned. Though the general office atmosphere was focused and busy, relationships were comfortably informal. Zeitlin said, "Massimo had an amazing ability to distill meaning and Lella made it happen, with attention to detail and the daily routine of seeing things through. There was a great energy, a healthy, visceral atmosphere in the office," he said. "There was always lively banter. He was handsome; she was beautiful and elegant. The women were a little in love with Massimo and the men were in love with Lella, and because everyone had a soft spot, it drove the office." [14]

The office sometimes seemed like a big family, and lunch was a communal time with almost everyone joking and laughing together. Sometimes they laughed at Massimo. "He can develop obsessions," said Caterina Roiatti. "At one point they were working on a showroom and Massimo wanted to put a tortellini bar at the top, just because he loved to say 'tortellini bar.'" [15] Massimo does enjoy pasta, and he is content with consistency in menus as much as in design. "He had a period of tortellini and brodo [broth] for lunch. It lasted for days," [16] said Laura Hillyer. Sometimes Massimo would be in the kitchen as the workday was ending, preparing salami and pouring Prosecco or making drinks, encouraging everyone to relax and be together. In the meantime, Lella was advising, encouraging, and sometimes chastising the life or work decisions of young people in the office.

Donovan said, "Massimo could be mercurial, but I always felt confident with Lella—if a project was on shaky ground, she could put it into perspective." [17] Zeitlin said Lella could be the mercurial one. "She'd be angry and screaming at me, but five minutes later she'd call me a pet name. We would just keep working." In 1986 he started his own business. "Everything I do is because of the Vignellis," Zeitlin said. "That is the only thing I knew; the only experience I had. The Vignelli experience is so strong, it is hard to break away to consider things differently." [18]

Donovan left Vignelli Associates to begin teaching, then opened his own studio a few years later; doing so gave him an even greater appreciation for all that Lella did. Balancing professional goals and a job with the demands of home and family often was, and is, complicated for women. Men are not immune to this, but typically women bear the brunt of work and worry for the family. Lella was no exception, as she mothered their two young children, managed the household, kept a watchful eye on business and financial records, and still maintained her own creative career.

"Lella was the people person who understood the human relationships and how people worked together. She established the overall attitude of the office," said Hillyer. "When I think about Lella, I think of elegance, style, determination—the typical fierce determination of stubborn mountain people. Massimo is gaiety, creativity, fun… Sure, there would be bickering sometimes but their relationship—our relationship—was a blend of friendship, devotion, and professional focus on what we were doing." [19]

Lella was respected for her ability to multitask long before that term was widely used. She set the agenda for their lives. "It wasn't that easy, but I survived," she said. "I wanted to focus on my work, but I couldn't totally. Many times I didn't trust myself; I was tired; I couldn't think straight."

Vignelli Kids: Luca and Valentina

Luca and Valentina grew up with insights and advantages as Vignelli children; design and creative thinking were part of the air they breathed. As kids, they liked being in the office. "There were plenty of art supplies: every color marker and paper, and French curves and all the circle templates. Everybody in the office was fun; they were all young and cool," said Luca. Valentina said, "Our friends would come to our house—they thought it was so futuristic, but we were used to it. Most people assumed that the attitude toward our living space was 'don't touch this—you are going to break it.' No, the furniture and objects were there to use—but with respect. You didn't need to break the springs on the sofa, but if you wanted to build a house with the sofa pillows, go ahead."

"My sister and I grew up as 'free-range chickens,'" said Luca. "We would see our parents first thing in the morning and then in the evening when they came home for dinner. They worked all the time, but they would always take a phone call from us, at any age, any time." Valentina laughed at Luca's description of their childhood. She agreed with him. "We had a procession of nannies because our parents were working," she said. "Our dinner was at eight o'clock, not at six o'clock like most Americans, because that's when they got home and also, that is Italian." Dinner was a family time, although conversation was often about work because it was not a separate part of life. Luca said, "They would continue their conversations from work, and sometimes their arguments from work, around the table. It was important for the family to be together, but it wasn't 'how was your day at school?'"

Their understanding of their parents evolved as they grew. Luca said, "One thing that was fun as a kid was that their designs were popular. I would go to a friend's house and they would have the Heller dishes, or maybe the Heller Pyrex. Or I would ride on the subways and say 'my dad did that [signage].' In a sense it helped me communicate who my parents were, and what they did, to my friends—they could see their stuff on the street, they could see the design of Bloomingdale's, they carried lunch to school in a Bloomingdale's bag."

The Vignellis were a regular part of the New York art scene. The family went to the Castelli Gallery almost every weekend. The kids grew up going to showrooms, SoHo galleries and Warhol's Factory. They attended openings at MoMA and the Guggenheim. Even as young children, they accompanied their parents to parties. Valentina said, "I remember being at Jack Larsen's [textile] showroom when I was about five, which is funny because I worked for him much later. So we always knew all this design; we eventually realized not everyone's parents did that, but someone's got to do it. I think I was in fourth grade when we had our picture in the *New York Times Magazine*. [20] That was certainly exciting. We had 'design through osmosis.' When we got older and also started to go into design, it was really nice to have dinner with Richard Meier or Philip Johnson and to be inspired by that person."

Luca said, "They were very, very driven, but they did care about family. They let us be ourselves. Massimo would typically play classical music, but if I put on music, he was okay with whatever I chose. It could be anything from The Beatles to Hendrix—they bought every Beatles record—or if Hendrix came on they would say, 'we saw him at Woodstock.'"

Luca's early interest in photography developed into a professional focus as he matured. He liked helping the designers with their production tasks. "When I was ten or eleven, I learned to use the 3M machine and the Photostat booth. They would ask 'do you want to Photostat this?' Yes! I loved going into that little darkroom," he said. Luca had a complete photographic darkroom in the Tenth Avenue office. He shot photos for some client projects; he shot portraits of his parents and documented many of the Vignelli products, so his images were often published and credited. Over time, his parents realized their good fortune in having a photographer in the family; compared to many other designers, the Vignelli archives are more fully documented because of Luca's work.

"Our parents had really cool friends: designers and photographers," said Luca. "One of Dad's best friends from his youth was Mario Caligiuri. He was going to photograph the construction of the World Trade Center, and he invited me to come along. I was probably eight. It was amazing! When I was older and got more into photography, I started assisting them: Mario Caligiuri, Henry Wolf—that was great for a kid."

Luca and Valentina didn't idolize their parents, but they respected them and they learned from them. They also took critiques to heart. "I remember trying linoleum printmaking at school and then getting some linoleum as a Christmas present," said Valentina. "The first thing I did? My mom thought it was terrible, so I didn't do any more. I dropped it—I was probably eleven or twelve. It certainly made an impression when my parents said 'not good.' It could be difficult, but it didn't necessarily scare me off from doing something that interested me. Our family dynamic wasn't necessarily that of a traditional family; it was four people who worked together." For awhile, Valentina moved a desk into a closet in her room, imitating the hidden cupboards she saw in her parents' office. She could simply close the door on any mess and avoid conflicts about neatness.

Like her brother, Valentina also began working in the office as she grew up, helping as a receptionist and later assisting with graphic design production. "I would do freelance work in the office when I needed extra cash," she said. "My father would give me a book project, and I could immediately interpret it because his drawings were so exact. Back then, we were still doing mechanicals, but it came so easily to me that I could complete the work very quickly."

Valentina eventually studied textile design at Rhode Island School of Design (RISD). She said, "In design school, I would drive my teachers crazy. They could see that whatever the problem was, I came up with one of the best solutions in class. They could also see that I'd worked perhaps one hour on it when other people worked much longer. It would make them nuts, but that was the way I had learned to approach work. My approach to work was influenced by my parents: find the most straightforward solution—not necessarily simple, but appropriate—and do it the best you can. Start with a good idea and go for it. I learned a certain decisiveness that a lot of people lack; I learned how to quickly scrap an idea that didn't work, and how to stick with a good idea and use it effectively."

As they matured, Luca and Valentina heard or read criticism of their parents. They learned to take it in stride; often comments were simply a different professional point of view. One example of this was presented in *ID* magazine, May 1983. Author Steven Holt wrote, "To the degree that he meets the Bauhaus ideal of obliterating the distinctions between graphics, products, and interiors, Vignelli has been successful in his equal treatment of two- and three-dimensional design… But by the same token, much of Vignelli's design seems to neglect the particular qualities of an object or idea in favor of whatever underlying characteristics may be shared amongst the various designs and their media… Despite his current claims to have saturated his design philosophy with issues of ambiguity, appropriateness, and discipline, Vignelli's work, whether in two dimensions or three, fundamentally centers around a search for and imposition of structure."[21]

Many would argue that structure is a manifestation of discipline. And many would agree with the Vignellis: in a world that is often chaotic and confusing, the imposition of clarity through structure is appropriate and welcomed. Acceptance of that line of reasoning was, not surprisingly, one of the characteristics that led to success for anyone who worked in the Vignelli office. Openness to that idea brought a consistent flow of clients and work to the office as well.

The Other "Vignelli Kids"

Back in the days of Unimark, young designers often described it as "Unimark University," in part because of what they learned from Massimo. That continued at Vignelli Associates. Bill Freeman, who worked in Unimark's New York office, said, "Massimo brought a sense of professionalism with him to New York that I had not experienced before. At Yale, the concept of professionalism was stressed in the abstract, but Massimo did this in very practical ways. The fact that he believed in a logical and functional approach to design, and that his work fit within a long tradition of European design contrasted with the state of American design of the early sixties. Most young American designers, like me, were adrift in a sea of eclecticism. Most American designers would do many, many sketches and then try to compress and combine them. At Unimark, Massimo's approach was 'do one very good one.' I chose to follow Massimo and adopted an approach to design similar to his."[22]

Throughout their careers, Lella and Massimo have been teachers, mentors, and role models to the many young people in their office. They accepted this responsibility willingly. Professors sent their best design students to New York. Most of the students described their Vignelli experience as a seminal period of professional growth. Massimo and Lella would regularly walk through the studio, looking over people's shoulders and discussing the developing work. Their criticisms could be harsh, but they were equally clear in announcing successes and sharing excitement over good work.

"Lella and Massimo were surrogate parents for me," said Michael Bierut. He began working at Vignelli Associates in June 1980. "There was so much that I needed to learn about culture. I was from suburban Cleveland; unworldly, untraveled… I couldn't even fathom the breadth of their views. They knew all the names in music, art, architecture. I was constantly going to the library or to Massimo's books; I did not know how big the world was. They weren't collecting culture, as in studying old photos or books—it was much more primal. Clients were all transformed by being with the Vignellis." So were the young designers. Bierut said, "Vignelli Associates was a master and apprentice setup. You never saw that they intended to nurture; you would just 'get it.'" [23]

Jonathan Wajskol was a student of Massimo's at Parsons School of Design in 1980, and not long after graduating he joined Vignelli Associates. "Massimo was a wonderful teacher," said Wajskol. "He set a tremendous example by taking a stand, by not making concessions. With him there is no negotiation; things must be done a certain way with clear objective and a clear idea of the outcome. Massimo was a powerful influence for me." [24]

"The times were interesting—on the street, in the marketplace, in life—it was a mess and there was a contrary sentiment in the air," said Wajskol. "Memphis [post-modernism, New Wave] came to New York in 1983. Massimo was the antithesis of that." If that contrary spirit rose in the office, it rarely lasted for long because it simply did not fit. Wajskol was friends with Austrian designer Christoph Radl. Radl developed graphics for Sottsass Associati, the leading Memphis group in Milan. "We were looking at some notes and Christoph separated each point with a wavy line. That intrigued me," Wajskol said. "Later, Lella asked me to prepare a memo for her and I divided the topics with a squiggly line. She was appalled. 'What does it mean, this wiggly line? Do it right, do it professionally!' I was still so inexperienced; I underestimated the implication that a little line could have—it was almost like I was a traitor. For me, that was a revealing moment in thinking about rational versus non-rational design." Ironically, soon after that Massimo was asked to design materials for the launch of Memphis in the United States. Michael Bierut took the lead on that project for the office.

Massimo said, "The people we see, who come to see us, are the best from all over the world. Top designers, major architects—names that are legends for design kids—this was part of everyday life in the office." Michael Donovan said, "There was a constant stream of Italian architects and designers: Gae Aulenti, Cini Boeri, Sergio Asti, Mario Bellini, Marco Zanuso… That close connection to Europe was a benefit for us." [25] Leading American architects, and international business and cultural leaders were also regular visitors. Young designers realized that their knowledge of the world was limited, but it grew quickly through association with the Vignellis.

Designer Graham Hanson said, "Massimo mostly taught by example—by his actions, by the way he responded to things. He always knew where to go with a problem, promoting the familiar phrase from protégés: 'What would Massimo do?' His solutions, on the surface, appeared to be quite simple, but when you broke them down and dissected them, they were remarkably intelligent and full of nuanced complexities. These were part of the disciplined logic that underpinned all of his work; they stayed out of the way, but added ease and interest, and the combination of simplicity and complexity made his work unique, timeless, and elegant. Designers used to come and go from the office based on their ability to pick up on this approach. Massimo would say, 'They either get it right away, or they never get it at all,' and he had very little patience for lack of understanding or aptitude." [26]

Hanson also learned from Lella. He said, "In Lella's mind, the solution to everything was so simple and obvious that it really only required disciplined execution. She was not patient with exploration, which was understandable with her level of experience. Additionally, she saw things more eloquently from a business perspective and understood the importance of executing projects efficiently. This was especially important given the large scale of many of the projects that came through the office. She was not particularly favorable to highly conceptual solutions. She favored the elegant, geometrical, logical solutions that were formed through restraint, rigor, and pragmatism. Her work illustrates that the approach is effective. Furthermore, it has proven to be highly influential."

Sharon Singer worked closely with Lella for fourteen years. She said, "I was in Chicago in 1986 and got to know Guido Buratto at the Artemide showroom, so when I wanted to move to New York he called Lella Vignelli to see if she needed anyone. At the interview, she was hard to understand and 'the palace' [office] was intimidating, but she said, 'I can see you think like we do,' and I was hired. At the beginning we would go to meet clients together. She would tell clients exactly what she thought, and she was good at pinpointing the issues, but she never lost her accent—she didn't want to lose it. One time during her presentation, a client whispered to me, 'Do you understand what she is saying? You will have to tell me later.' Lella was always pushing us to find new materials, and her ideas came out of the materials. She was very decisive, but she was more willing than Massimo to let others handle the details. She trusted me and I was proud of that." [27]

The lessons that people learned sometimes weren't about design. Singer said, "Lella thought of all of us as her kids and she encouraged us to be balanced. If we were working late and I wanted to go to the gym, she would encourage me to go." Janice Carapellucci remembered driving with Massimo to a client meeting. They listened to an opera while they traveled. "Though we were already late when we arrived, the opera wasn't quite over, so, very slowly, Massimo drove a lap around the client's parking lot, waiting for Pavarotti to sing his last note. I will never forget his impish grin of defiance and pleasure. Lesson learned? Art first—always." [28]

Designers learned from each other as well. "Generally speaking, Massimo would work with more senior staff, and the senior staff would work with junior staff," said designer Yoshiki Waterhouse. "But that's not entirely true— if there was a project that he really enjoyed, he would sit with any of us. My office was next to Rebecca Rose and she was my go-to person if I needed advice. I also loved talking to David Law. He was enormously talented and very busy, but he was generous with his time. He would sit with you, enunciating his words carefully, choosing his words wisely. He would make it perfectly clear how a drawing ought to be; how to write detailed specifications." [29]

Designer Lev Zeitlin also learned from David Law. Zeitlin's first task as an intern at Vignelli Associates was to research and prepare a feasibility study for the handkerchief chair. Zeitlin's educational background was in industrial design so the actual research wasn't difficult, but he had no experience with graphic design. Once he gathered the data, it was Law who guided him in designing the actual proposal. Law explained typographic hierarchy, the use of the grid, rules as dividing elements—the Vignelli structure that was known through client work was equally a part of the internal functioning of the office. No letter, no document, was presented casually.

"David sat in his cubicle and he was like a genie; when you let him out, things happened!" said Zeitlin. "He was patient and willing to explain minute details. He was my school; he knew so much. He was an amazing craftsman too. He built the prototype of the handkerchief chair by hand. It was fascinating to see because the craftsmanship was incredible." [30] Intended as a tribute to Paolo Venini, the chair was inspired by Venini's handkerchief vase, which was popular in the 1950s. The chair is now produced by Knoll.

Robert Traboscia said, "I learned what design meant at Vignelli. I am a low-key construction guy; good with tradespeople and contractors. Vignelli Associates was filled with bright lively people talking the language of design, so I learned by observation, by listening. I am proud to be a descendant of Massimo and Lella. Rationale, aesthetics, problem-solving—I do things the same way. The Vignellis are about telling clear stories; their language is universal. I think the Vignellis are designers for the people, not for the masses, but for those in the know." [31]

Sharon Singer said Lella trusted the designers and gave them room to work independently. "At the beginning, we would go to meet clients together, but then I would make it happen and keep the clients happy," said Singer. "Massimo liked having a finger in everything and a lot of people did not like having so much direction. Lella was more willing to let others handle details. However, Lella could get exasperated with interns; if they did not do things properly, it frustrated her." [32]

The designers learned how to deliver effective presentations, whether on paper or in person. They learned that it wasn't enough to simply execute a solution; they needed skills in delivery as well. Massimo's approach to planning and staging involved a mix of attitude and style, brought to life by his genuine excitement at showing something new to an awaiting client. A stack of mounted drawings was placed face down on the table. Michael Bierut described the scene. "Massimo would rest his fingertips on the top board. He would look around the room and pause as if to control an almost uncontainable excitement. Then, unable to wait a second longer, Massimo would burst out, 'Wait until you see what we have for you today. It's fantastic!' A carefully wrought presentation would follow, but for much of the audience the sale was already rung up. 'My God,' you could see them thinking, 'if this guy is so sure, who are we to argue?'" [33]

Massimo and Lella speak fondly of the young designers in the office, and there were many of them over the years. "They belonged," Massimo said. "They learned our design discipline, our lifestyle and behavior; they saw the security and dignity of our position. It is osmosis. Young people are discovering affinities, shaping their lives; that is the most important thing. They absorb mannerisms: the music playing in the office, the way we dress, the way we talk with clients. This is a certain attention to elegance, despising vulgarities. It is intellectual elegance that comes from the mind, not from outside. The way the office is well designed, the strong ethics—they pay attention to this. When they go on their own, they carry that influence."

Each of the interviewed designers spoke of meaningful lessons, large and small. Design was only part of this. Learning about operating a business was also important because after leaving the Vignellis, many of the designers opened their own businesses. "Lella taught me to have no fear," said Sharon Singer about the often uncomfortable topic of establishing prices. While preparing for a meeting with a client, Lella described the scope of the project and the price she intended to set for doing the work. Singer said, "Lella was good at pinpointing what a client needed. They were decisive, they were fair, and they knew what their work was worth." Little lessons were equally memorable. "One time I wore something new to the office. After a meeting, Lella told me that I clashed with the conference room," said Singer. "After that, I don't think I ever wore anything with a loud pattern."

Long hours and hard work were expected, but Lella and Massimo simply expected full commitment from everyone, themselves included. Designer Rocco Piscatello began working at Vignelli Associates in 1991. He said, "It was a busy place. Groups of people were always coming through the office. Lella never got off the phone, and Massimo couldn't stop working. They were out every night at meetings, and they never passed up an opportunity to do interviews. So many times we would hear Lella saying, 'Massimo! We have to leave—we are late! Give it to the kid, he's good. [This, over time, referred to various designers including Bierut and Piscatello.] We have to go now!'" [34] The design staff realized these actions created new opportunities, but they also knew it was exhausting.

Lella said, "I think we've had a good life, so far. Fatiguing, for sure, because we've worked so hard. But we have the life we wanted and I am very lucky to feel that way." [35] Lella told people that she never wanted to stop working. She was not opposed to slowing down—eventually—but living a busy and full life was part of the plan for both of them.

Reviewing construction plans for the Minneapolis Museum of Fine Arts, 1974.

The Tenth Avenue office of Vignelli Associates, 1985.

The Showcase Office: Tenth Avenue

In 1984, the Vignellis signed a fifteen-year lease and began a total renovation for their new headquarters on Tenth Avenue. Quietly functional and visually stunning, the new office showcased their confidence and light-hearted sophistication to everyone who stepped off the elevator on the fourteenth floor. Lella's appreciation for diverse materials and their textures, colors, and characteristics resulted in a space that was far from ordinary. Lead panels, corrugated sheets of galvanized steel, sandblasted glass, gold leaf, particle board, and plates of raw steel created contrasts of dull, matte, gloss, and translucent surfaces. The office was flooded in daylight from skylights above and huge windows all around. "We used ordinary materials in extraordinary ways; we wanted to show how simple materials can be noble through their use and their environment," said Lella. "You have to see materials and know what you can do with them. And you have to know what is too much."

Paul Sachner critiqued the interior in *Architectural Record* in 1986. He noted that the designers "articulated the space with a selection of materials that exhibits a typically Vignellian combination of playfulness and control. There is an intentionally mannerist quality in the unorthodox application of such prosaic materials as corrugated galvanized steel on the back wall of the design studio and, in Lella Vignelli's office suite, particle-board walls—stained white and finished with clear flat lacquer—that mimic cut stone… Minimalist or not, they know exactly where they stand on the continuing debate among Modernists and Postmodernists: 'We are happy Miesians,' exclaims Massimo assuredly. 'More is a bore.' As I left their tranquil aerie and began my trek back to Rockefeller Center, I could see his point." [1]

Nearly everyone in the office was involved during the months of construction and preparation. Valentina said, "My parents had close relationships with many people in the office, and when we moved to the new space, Luca and I—and all the kids in the office—were there doing the detailing." At the time of the move, Vignelli Associates had about thirty employees and interns. The company continued to grow for several more years, until the 1990s when the proliferation of desktop computers streamlined many design production tasks and a gradual downsizing made sense.

Massimo, typically, was impatient with the construction process and eager to have everything in place. He said, "I was getting nervous because it was taking so much time, but eventually it was all done beautifully." From various angles, Vignelli Associates had views of the Hudson River, the Statue of Liberty, the New Jersey Palisades, and the skyline of Manhattan. With a Hudson River scene outside and smartly organized space within, Lella's office was known as "The Salon," in part because sometimes her back bothered her and then she abandoned her desk. Lella revived seventeenth-century salon tradition by "receiving her guests" from a reclining position on the large Saratoga sofa. "I went to the doctor and he recommended bed rest, but I put myself on the sofa. People would meet with me there. When the work is there, you just have to do it," she said.

Valentina said, "Mom did the hiring and firing, but she also gave pep talks when someone wasn't doing so well." "Who did I fire?" protested Lella. "You fired me!" said Valentina. They laugh about it now, remembering the long-ago battle between a headstrong teen and an overworked mother. Obviously all is forgiven. "I would say, 'Listen to me—step it up,'" Lella said, laughing. "But it was not always bad news when they came to me!"

While Massimo focused upon a person's portfolio, Lella focused on the person, evaluating character and personality. Valentina explained, "She knew there was a pool of employees and everyone had to work together. She would consider: can we work with this person, can they learn from us? Can we learn from them?" Sometimes she took complete control of the interviewing process. "Lella hired me," said designer Rocco Piscatello. "I didn't even meet with Massimo until after I was hired." [2]

Massimo's office looked out to the midtown skyline. His window framed the distinctive Art Deco spire of the Chrysler Building, but most visitors were focused inside as they sought time and attention at his desk. (It was actually a table, designed as part of the new office. It hasn't changed in the years since, except for the addition of a computer and an iPad.) Its surface was a thick square slab of darkened raw steel. A neat stack of white paper was aligned and ready for use. A taboret next to his chair held other necessary tools—his favorite soft-lead pencil (Swiss made Caran d'Anche 3mm mechanical pencil with a red cap and 4B lead), China markers in just the right red, erasers—

minimal equipment to produce maximum results. That desk was notable for the quantity of work that came from it—and for its cleanliness.

Yoshimi Kono said, "I worked at that table so many times, sketching and talking. Those were always the best moments. You have to ask, what is the essence of design? You have to ask, what is life for? I think that Massimo understands that every product is designed for humans, for feeling better in your life." [3] Kono shared a story about designing a water fountain for a Poltrona Frau showroom. The look of the fountain was not the starting point for design, because Massimo led him into the kitchen. Kono said, "He started stacking cups and turned on the water, playing with the distance and the flow. He asked me, 'What is the sound?' If the distance was too far, it sounded like peeing—it wasn't pleasant. By stacking more cups and changing the distance, the noise was different. Massimo focused on what was right—how it sounded, what seemed right to him. It was such a simple thing, but when others design a fountain, they don't go to the kitchen. He gets close to the work; he feels it. He surprises me because even as a minimalist, he can always find new ways to do things."

Finding new ways to do things was characteristic of both Massimo and Lella. Sharon Singer said, "Massimo would show you what he was thinking— hand him a napkin and he would draw. Lella was verbal in conveying ideas. She developed the overall language, the elements, for the Poltrona Frau showrooms. She had the vision of developing a 'kit of parts,' a series of wall systems that could translate to hanging, or floating, or as a backdrop in the showrooms. The work, like Massimo's two-dimensional work, was always based on a grid." [4]

The grid was particularly apparent in the Steelcase showroom in Grand Rapids, Michigan, in 1993. Singer said, "That showroom was a great collaboration between the two of them. It was like a brochure done in three dimensions," said Singer. "Lella created a system of perforated steel panels that we had bent into various curves and shapes. They were free-standing; they created an arc on the floor and samples would hang from them or drape over them. Part of the work was developing the idea, but then it was finding the materials, finding the people who could do the bending, the sandblasting, making the honeycomb perforations."

Designer Rebecca Rose said, "It was always a joyful experience to sit at Massimo's desk and participate in the creation of an elegant solution to the problem at hand… Sometimes this occurred during a meeting with the client. At other times it was just the two of us, talking and drawing, questioning assumptions, exploring and discarding ideas and approaches, and celebrating that wonderful moment when the solution became clear. Once Massimo completed the final set of pencil drawings, he would hand them to me to implement, and his desk would be clear again."[5]

Few people are as disciplined as Massimo, who has little patience for visible disorganization and clutter. Rose found herself caught between the Vignelli desire for order and neatness and the reality of working on long-lasting architectural graphics projects, which meant keeping materials for months and sometimes years. She wasn't the only designer who was chastised for a messy work area. When he reached his limit of tolerance, Massimo would confront culprits directly, or they would return to find a note in his unmistakable handwriting, emphatically requesting that the clutter be cleaned up.

Though the Vignellis believed in design as a tool for the public good, they didn't usually seek out government projects. These often involved a different sort of clutter. Neither Lella nor Massimo had much patience for the bureaucratic red tape and reams of paperwork that seemed inevitably to be part of such work. However, a widespread downturn in design business put everyone in the office on the lookout for new client opportunities. In the early 1990s, a deep and global recession created challenges for all sorts of businesses. Vignelli Associates was diverse and adaptable, but it was not an easy time.

"Corporate and institutional clients are squeezing their suppliers to compensate for their own dismal revenue outlook," wrote Willam P. Dunk in *Graphis,* November 1990.[6] The editors in *Print Regional Design Annual* in July 1991 also noted the effects of recession, writing that graphic designers have "learned to cushion the impact of bad times by extending their expertise to related areas of design, and some are evolving a tougher-minded, Darwinian attitude toward their chosen specialty: Survival of the fittest is what it's really all about, they say, and they'd better get used to it."[7]

Vignelli Associates was invited to partner with an architectural team on renovations for New York's Grand Central Terminal. Part of the required paperwork was an Equal Employment Opportunity Commission (EEOC) statement. The Vignellis did not have one. Janice Carapellucci said, "If you looked around the office, it was obvious that they did not discriminate—it was a United Nations in there!" Yoshimi Kono agreed. "When I was there, we had Russian, Dutch, French, and Spanish designers. I'm Japanese. Everyone was speaking their own language, so it was wonderful—nicely diversified. Language was not so important; we could see and draw and understand,"[8] he said.

Despite having a compliant atmosphere, the EEOC statement was a necessary part of the process. Carapellucci was writing proposals during this period. Her steadfast persistence—and her understanding of the Vignellis—was as valuable as her organizational ability. Carapellucci asked the architect to share a sample version. "He sent an EEOC statement from a smaller engineering firm. It was four pages long," she said. "The Vignellis are very conscious of language. Their approach is: say only what is needed. They would never want four pages, so I created 'our' statement using only the first paragraph and the last paragraph from that example. I typed it and took it to Lella for her signature. She took one look and said, 'it is too long,' and crossed out one paragraph. I retyped it and took it to Massimo to sign. The architect laughed when he saw it."[9] The Vignelli office did develop new signage for Grand Central Terminal and the project was a success.

Clients most often came to the Vignellis through personal connections and referrals. Lella and Massimo were smart, engaging, logical, and reliable. The Vignellis were practical problem-solvers with an approach that added, as they often said, "a sense of ambiguity," in part because it was not readily identifiable to a particular time. The Vignellis did not decorate; extraneous material and surface pattern had no place in their solutions. Their work was refined, yet it often displayed a hint of whimsy too. That usually came from Massimo. A design intern, Daisy Ames, said, "Massimo looks at ordinary things and sees a design inspiration. Even though he preaches against the vulgarity surrounding us, he searches for the beauty first. He is constantly absorbing information and searching for its appropriate application."[10]

Designer Beatriz Cifuentes once shared a package of licorice in the studio, offering a piece of the candy to Massimo. Ames said, "Massimo accepted, but squinted, raised the piece to eye level, rotated it, held it over his head, then at arm's length. Then he asked for more. He placed four pieces of licorice on the desk vertically. Then he skipped off to get a piece of paper and slowly lowered it to rest squarely on top of the four pieces. 'Ah! It's a table, is it not?' We laughed. 'You see the twisting, the thickness—they make fine table legs!'

He swooped up the items which were no longer items of consumption, but his new tools for design, and said, 'OK, I'm going to draw it.' Then he raced off to his desk."

The Vignellis constantly observe their environment. They readily imagine multiple interpretations, filtering information for its potential in illuminating problems and defining solutions. It's been part of their success from the beginning. Surveying the disheveled end of a dinner party led to the concept of "a clean pile of dirty dishes," and the award-winning 1964 design of stacking melamine dinnerware, which made clearing the table a more pleasant task. The Vignellis worked on packaging for Nine Flags men's cologne in 1967. Gillette asked for "masculine" containers, sending samples of the scents to the Unimark office in standard chemical flasks. Massimo simply adapted that flask, then the set of nine fragrances was packed for retail sale in a Styrofoam shipping container. (Although the packaging was attention-getting, there was a lack of repeat buyers once they smelled the cologne, he said.) In 1979, the domes of Venetian churches inspired the shapes of Ciga glassware. Very little escapes their attention as the Vignellis think about ways to make life more pleasant, efficient, elegant.

Rather than lament troubling economics in the 1990s, they simply broadened their design explorations in multiple directions, including clothing. It was another manifestation of their mantra, "If you can't find it, design it." Borne out of frustration with the fashion industry, this wasn't a totally new investigation, because Massimo had designed some of his own clothing as a teenager. Lella and Massimo also developed a clothing collection in 1977 but never pursued its licensing. Now their thinking was more serious. "We were not making *fashion,* which is transitory and based on the idea of obsolescence. We were making *clothing* with a purpose: to protect and follow the body. We grew tired of being fashion victims," said Massimo. They built production space, and a showroom for a Vignelli-designed clothing collection, inside the Vignelli Associates office.

Fashion History According to Massimo

"Examine the silliness of fashion. Length is either too long or too short, lapels are always too wide or too narrow, pocket placement makes no sense, pleats and creases are difficult to iron, cuffs are a repository for dust, and too many buttons!" he said. Massimo is obsessive in thinking about buttons. While talking, he sketched a history of men's fashion to emphasize how clothing relates to its own period.

His observations were uniquely humorous. "Of course, Adam and Eve started with the fig leaves, and the Romans had draped togas," he said. "Look at the Dark Ages—no cleaners and plenty of chickens, shit, and mud, so the fabrics were dark and heavy. The Renaissance was fabulous, and stayed so until into the 1500s. Pilgrims were serious and pious, so their long coats had lots of buttons. It took time to get out of that coat, and by the time they did, their passions were cooled. Revolutionary times also had lots of buttons so they'd behave, even on the cuffs to prevent them from wiping their noses on their sleeves. The eighteenth century had a great silhouette. There were still lots of buttons, but the coats were unbuttoned—they were ready! The end of the Civil War had a natural shoulder; it was democracy versus aristocracy. Then the English ruled fashion in the Edwardian time. It was spiffy with strong lines and creases, but they had servants to take care of ironing. In 1936, after the New Deal, it was an optimistic era in America. Then the shoulders were natural but wide, like bridges spanning a river. The 1960s Brooks Brothers was button-down, regimental, creased. In the 1980s, Armani invented the unconstructed men's suit: wide, soft, no lines or creases."

That explanation led into the 1990s, describing Vignelli clothing for men and women: nothing unnecessary, easy construction, pockets only on the seams. Massimo said, "It takes sixty-four pieces to make a traditional jacket, but only ten to make ours. We use the same fabric for a jacket and a sweater/shirt so it becomes one thing visually. It is a program, a wardrobe plan." Initially seamstresses who worked in the office made the clothing, and later the fabrics were sent to Miami to be cut and assembled.

Lella said, "The design was very simple, so the beauty lay in the selection of materials, which is where I think it should be. The fabrics were amazing. The men's collection came in black, blue, and gray, and the fabrics were wool, cotton, and linen. For women we had the same three colors plus red and camel. The women's clothes were made from more feminine materials like silk and linen… We had terrific coats, made out of cashmere with a very high collar that partially covered the face and deep pockets for your hands."[11]

"Dispensing with architectonic shoulders, regimental sleeve buttons, and those pesky but significant lapels… the collarless, elastic-waisted Vignelli look mixes 'Space 1999' with a hint of Mao, a dash of Courrèges, and just a whiff of constructivism," Andrew Olds wrote in *ID* in 1991. "At the same time, its prevalent blacks and grays conjure up something undeniably clerical. 'You look like a priest, but that's OK,' laughs Vignelli. The Design:Vignelli label offers design-conscious (not fashion-conscious) consumers a garment of dramatic simplicity." [12] The clothing showroom, like the conference areas in the Vignelli Associates office, had gridded sand-blasted glass walls. A large mirror was the dramatic element in the space; a changing room was behind it, with simple racks of clothing to the side. The clothing models for promotional materials were all Vignelli employees. Lella and Massimo sometimes modeled the clothing too.

With a resurgence of other design business, Design:Vignelli clothing became less of a priority, but still Lella and Massimo considered expanding the clothing operation. They designed store plans that included tags and boxes, chairs, tables, and fitting rooms for a total coordination of product, space, and graphics. Massimo said, "We tried to have someone manufacture and sell for us, but that did not work well. The manufacturers were all afraid that since the clothing was so simple, it would be too quickly copied and they would not be able to recoup their investment." Design:Vignelli was sold in the Vignelli office for ten years, until the Tenth Avenue office was closed. For awhile it was also available in a boutique in Barney's on Seventh Avenue, at Luminaire in Chicago, and in a small store in Paris. The qualities that made the clothing effective are timeless—comfort, ease, elegant simplicity—projecting a sense of ambiguous style rather than being a definable fashion trend. Massimo, Lella, and a few close friends continue to wear Design:Vignelli clothes.

To be fully clothed means, for many people, adding some embellishments that are functional, or fun, or both. The Vignellis attended to that as well by espousing simple geometric forms and sophisticated materials. Together they developed watches for Junod in Switzerland. Their watch faces, not surprisingly, are minimal: no numerals; the hour and minute noted merely by straight linear hands; seemingly floating atop bands of smooth black leather. One is a dual time watch. "It is for people, like me, who constantly travel in different time zones and need to remember both times," said Massimo. Another, the Halo Watch, displays Vignelli playfulness through a "halo" that surrounds the black face. The interchangeable halo rings are available in different hues of anodized aluminum, allowing a wearer to customize and change the look of the watch without diminishing the integrity of its design.

Lella created jewelry. One necklace developed from their studies of fashion history as she reinterpreted an Elizabethan ruff collar in silver. The Sensa Fine necklace was a completely different approach, with hinged arcs of silver tubing allowing multiple forms to be made from a single necklace. Sometimes coiled and compact, at other times it sensuously curved down the body of the wearer. She designed a bracelet to match. Numerical rings made a bold statement in silver as well, conceived as commemorative items that would be a welcome and useable alternative to clunky awards gathering dust on a shelf. These were all produced by San Lorenzo in Italy. "If something is really good, it will last," said Lella. "We try to find better solutions; we do not like trends." The accessories, as well as furniture and housewares, were products of Vignelli Design. Lella managed that work while Massimo was in charge of Vignelli Associates.

The Vignellis often had a transformative effect on people's ideas and attitudes. Friends and clients alike found that spending time with Lella and Massimo almost inevitably changed the way they looked at the world. Like many, Nancy Olnick and Giorgio Spanu began as clients, became friends, and in the process found their thinking and actions to be forever altered. In 2000, the couple were preparing their collection of twentieth-century Murano glass for exhibition at what was then the American Craft Museum. (In 2002 the name changed to the Museum of Arts and Design.) Curator David Revere McFadden suggested talking to the Vignellis about the exhibition design. "Everyone assumed we already knew the Vignellis," said Spanu, "but that did not happen until we went to their office to talk about this installation." [13]

"As we talked about our collection, and mentioned pieces by Carlo Scarpa, Massimo's face lit up," Olnick said. "I think we brought him back to a great time, a great experience in his life. He told us about his first job and about Paolo Venini. Then Lella and Massimo both left the office, telling us to wait. Maybe fifteen minutes later, Massimo came back with a three-dimensional maquette of the display cases, complete with drawn miniature pieces of glassware inside. We thought, 'Okay. That was easy. We're done.' That was the exhibit."

"I think it was special for them too because Luca did all of the photography— absolutely beautiful glass photography, the best we have seen. It was the first time for the three of them to work together as a family affair, so that was a bonus in the experience," said Spanu. The exhibit traveled around the

United States and to Milan over the next several years. The Vignellis adjusted the installation to fit each venue. Olnick said, "Lella was instrumental—so decisive on materials, so knowledgeable on costs—she was amazing at running their business. Massimo even helped to install the exhibit. He would hold the pieces like babies, and because they are jewels to us, we appreciated that."

The couples became close friends. The Vignellis often visited and enjoyed the gardens and the view from the Spanu home overlooking the Hudson River. Lella provided design input as they upgraded the property. When they were ready to build a new home on the site, they took Massimo's advice, selecting Spanish architect Alberto Campo Baeza. "We owe Lella and Massimo so much! Her thinking is crystal clear and he is a creative genius. Massimo arranged for us to meet Campo Baeza while he was on a sabbatical, teaching at Columbia. He came to our Manhattan apartment with the Vignellis. When he started talking, the warmth, the life, the spirit flowed; he has the same magical quality as Massimo," said Olnick.

Transition Again: The End of Tenth Avenue

In 2000, the lease expired on their Manhattan office. An article in *The New York Times* on September 28, 2000, noted that prohibitive rent was discouraging many lessees. "The severe shortage of office space and record rents are driving longtime New Yorkers out. One of the most prominent teams to go, Massimo and Lella Vignelli… made a painful decision to close their celebrated minimalist office at 475 Tenth Avenue when their fifteen-year lease expires next month. Rent on the space rose sixfold, to $62.50 a square foot." [14]

Massimo said, "It was a terrific space! I am glad that I got to experience it every day for fifteen years. However, we moved with the times. Since the office was designed for a manual working process, the space became redundant after we switched to computers. We went down to twenty-five employees, and later, by the time the lease expired, about fifteen. We really did not need the whole space any longer." The Vignellis considered staying, subletting part of their space to another business, but the notice of the substantial rent increase forced a realization: a new lease at Tenth Avenue was simply too expensive.

"We considered renting another space, but after the grandeur of Tenth Avenue, I could not adjust to an ordinary office, let alone subletting a space in someone else's office. That seemed like a demeaning and depressing alternative, so we decided to transform our apartment into an office/home," he said. Valentina said, "They were thinking that maybe they were at an age where they should retire—not really retire, but focus only on the projects that they wanted." Making that choice meant that they were forced to dramatically downsize the company. They gave notice to their entire staff. Though Lella and Massimo intended to continue working, it meant the end of Vignelli Associates as it had been for nearly thirty years.

When the Vignellis decided not to renew their lease at Tenth Avenue, they thought that the landlord would leave the office intact, using its functional beauty to entice a new lessee. Sadly, the building's owners declined that option, which made the emotional implications of this transition doubly difficult. Now they would be dismantling their respected professional team *and* their carefully designed space.

They rented a crane to transport heavy furnishings to the ground. Employees were invited to take elements from the office as the space was demolished. "It was hard to tear it apart. That office was the best; it was so big, so beautiful—it had everything we needed," said Lella. "It was hateful when it was destroyed. At the end, Massimo was upset and he couldn't do anything, not even moving the things from his own office. Luca had to take care of it." Massimo said, "It was very traumatic for me. As happens to me in those situations, I left without turning my head, pretending that a bomb destroyed the place." He approached changes in residence in the same way and had plenty of experience with that in his life.

Saying Goodbyes

As the office closed on Tenth Avenue, an entire group of designers set out for new opportunities, their resumes enhanced with the power of Vignelli credentials. Some, like Rocco Piscatello or Sharon Singer, opened their own firms, adding to the substantial list of businesses that emerged from the Vignelli experience. Yoshiki Waterhouse went to graduate school. Others found creative employment within existing firms. Singer said, "It was hard to think about going to work for someone else. I discussed it with Lella, because there were a few people I'd been working with and I wanted to continue working with them. Vignelli was a very hard act to follow so I went on my own. I think that most people ended up doing things on their own after that." [15]

Lella and Massimo recite a long list of strong designers, sensitive typographers, and capable project managers who came through their offices over the years. Designers are generally a mobile bunch, but many people stayed for years at Vignelli Associates. Working there did feel like being part of a family. It wasn't only Lella and Massimo who blurred the boundaries between personal and professional life, between individual and group experiences. Because of that, when other opportunities beckoned and good people left, it was difficult to say goodbye. After the goodbyes, the friendships continued.

A few partings were especially hard. Michael Bierut joined the Vignellis in 1980. Bierut specialized in graphic design, rising to vice president at Vignelli Associates. In 1990, he announced that he was leaving to become a partner at Pentagram. His relationship with Lella and Massimo had always been mutually supportive, filled with respect and genuine appreciation; he was widely and accurately regarded as the Vignelli heir apparent.

Jonathan Wajskol said, "Michael made a profound change in the office. He would persuade Massimo to give a breath of fresh air to the work—more current, younger in spirit. He was a strong influence." [16] Despite all that he had at Vignelli Associates, the excitement of new opportunities, and new tests of skill and direction was too strong for Bierut to resist. He said, "In 1990, I reached a point where I saw that I'd either work there for the rest of my life, or make a change... After a great deal of soul-searching, I decided to make the move. At that point I had worked at Vignelli Associates for one third of my life. Massimo and Lella were more than bosses to me—they were surrogate parents. Telling Massimo and Lella that I was leaving was probably the most painful thing I've ever done. When we actually had the talk, it was a relief for me and a bit of a shock for them, although I sense they must have seen it coming." [17]

Lella said, "Michael loved us, but he sensed that the two of us would be always strongly bound. The competition would be difficult because we are such a unit; we are too strong against another one." Massimo was gracious though devastated. "I raised him to be my successor, so when Michael said that he was going, it was traumatic. I felt I wasted a lot of effort—the plan I'd built up was thwarted by reality." Eventually all was forgiven and warm friendships continued.

Since that time, Bierut has often described the formative knowledge he gained at Vignelli Associates. In an article, "Battle Hymn of the Tiger Mentor,

Or, Why Modernist Designers Are Superior," he wrote, "By the time I left Vignelli Associates in 1990, I felt I was ready to move far beyond the limiting strictures of modernism. The period of graphic self-indulgence that followed is now a bit painful for me to contemplate. After a time I came to appreciate the tough love that my favorite mentor had so painstakingly administered for a full decade." [18]

Adapting to new realities and facing forward is one of Massimo's strong traits. He sighed at the memory of that parting, then smiled about the man he sometimes called "My Michael." "Of course it was hard at the time, but I am happy to hear Michael's positive mentions of the time with us and our formative effect on his career; that feels like some compensation for my efforts. We are now close again. I am happy to see his success. There are many that we are proud of, many who grew up in our office. Only Michael was traumatic, because most of the time when people were leaving, we were actually trying to reduce the size of the office."

Rocco Piscatello "replaced" Bierut, but he realized that in many ways, that was impossible to do. "After Michael left, Massimo was different. Of course he still expected strong employees to do strong work, but there wasn't interest in providing titled positions," said Piscatello. "Leaving the Vignellis is a difficult thing to do, but when you work for someone and it's time to leave, why not test the waters? I left when I was thirty, in 1997. It was hard to tell them, but I wanted to start my own firm. Lella was especially gracious. 'Listen, what you have is a once-in-a-lifetime opportunity. Do your own thing,' she said. So I did. Entrepreneurs are called risk-takers, but it's actually the reverse—to be an entrepreneur you have to learn to minimize risk, to have a plan. Lella and Massimo did that and with their encouragement, I did it too. I left them happy, and we are all still happy, still close." [19]

Lella and Massimo felt yet another loss deeply. For decades David Law had been an integral part of their lives and work. He retired when the Tenth Avenue office closed, then lost a battle with cancer, and passed away in 2003. Law had been a designer in Unimark's Chicago office. In 1973, he resigned along with four others to form the short-lived Design Planning Group, then he moved to New York to supervise the implementation of a Unimark-designed identity system at JCPenney. Law joined the Vignellis in about 1975, and from that point he contributed as a designer and project manager for many products: furniture, silver, china, and glass. Lella said, "David drew like Massimo, but he also had a different approach than Massimo because he worked in three dimensions; he always made mockups and models. He also helped me collect and organize the materials for the archives."

"David collaborated with me on the Fifty-third Street project [at Unimark], and from that occasion I had the opportunity to appreciate his care for details and his general design approach," said Massimo. "He was a hard worker with good knowledge of materials and processes. His approach was so close to mine that even his drawings were similar to mine. I couldn't distinguish between our drawings, and I'd have to ask him: did I draw that, or did you? Finally I had to put a mark on my work so I could tell. David was a terrific designer, one of the best at Unimark, and he developed all our products. He was a tremendous loss. I felt that it was almost like a transfer; like he didn't die, but he came into me. Like Lella, he was my partner. Of all the people we worked with, I was closest to him. I really miss him."

Lella and Massimo at RIT, 2005.

A. Sue Weisler

Inside the Vignelli home and office on East 67th Street, 2011.

Working From Home: East 67th Street

Once again, the Vignellis intertwined personal and professional life by combining home and office. Initially this decision seemed like it was imposed upon them by circumstances, not chosen with excitement. Michael Donovan, who has continued to be a close friend, knew that this transition was hard for them, but he wasn't surprised when they adapted and moved forward. He said, "The thing about Massimo and Lella is that they are both very rational. Logic works and Massimo takes great pride in using it." [1]

Although the Vignellis disparage the transitory nature of fashion, they are acutely conscious of style and visual impressions. Giving up the Tenth Avenue office worried Massimo because it had been an imposing space, but it quickly became obvious that their home office also created a positive impression for professional visitors. That shouldn't have surprised him, but seemingly it did. The Vignellis were social, hosting parties and gathering friends, so many people were familiar with their home. Their associations with it were already favorable. Newcomers entered and saw the dramatic leaded window, the art, the Vignelli furnishings, the sleek organization. They recognized a Vignelli sensibility in the spare and smart functionality, and they too were comfortable. Several people said that in some respects it was better than Tenth Avenue because it felt more personal.

"Our apartment became office during the day, home at night. Having a duplex made the transition easy. The bottom floor becomes office, the top floor is always residence; the whole thing is still grand and dignified. It did not look like a miserable home office. Gradually I got used to it and loved it, more than any other alternative," said Massimo. Most signficantly, he realized people were there to see him, to see Lella, and to seek strong solutions to their design problems. In that respect, nothing had changed.

The balance of projects between Vignelli Associates (graphic design and interiors), and Vignelli Design (products), stayed relatively consistent though there was a shift in their work. They had fewer corporate clients, which meant less emphasis on massive identity projects. Their aversion to middle management from the Unimark days continued ("They are people who are terrified of making mistakes," says Massimo), but that was rarely an issue for them. The Vignellis worked with company presidents and trusted decision-makers. Massimo and Lella continued to create most of their work based upon personal rapport, long-standing relationships, and shared affinities. They continued to be busy, and happy.

Lella was particularly satisfied as they settled into their home office. When the business was downsized, she had fewer administrative responsibilities. She could focus more on creative aspects of her projects and that realignment was well deserved. In addition, she was finally achieving individual recognition for her work, particularly the showrooms and interiors. "Now is the best time of my life," Lella said in 2009. "I enjoy working on products, because they are focused, but now I am doing the showrooms and they please me. I am traveling—I have fewer responsibilities with record-keeping, with home, with cooking. I am in control of myself; it is very different from the earlier years. Being older helps too."

Sometimes they paused to reflect on their accomplishments. "The greatest part of life for us has been growing together," said Lella. "In a relationship, it is important that you don't let yourself be taken over." She laughed, explaining, "I am practical. Massimo is creative even if what he is thinking is not always possible. We do our own projects, but we listen to each other."

A good leader has a sense of empathy and an ability to listen. Lella had both. "Massimo is purely about design—it is you, him, the project. Lella is a passionate pragmatist," said Michael Bierut. "She was the boss who called the shots on budgets, salaries, personnel—and she freed Massimo to drive his vision single-mindedly forward. She would be the first to interpret resistance from a client or to hear information that needed to be taken into consideration. 'Listen to what he is saying, Massimo,' she'd say." 2

"One of the dynamics that's important about the way they worked is that Lella created a shield around Massimo, where he was free to do his work. They were very critical of each other, so of course there were arguments," said Luca. One argument has become legendary. It rose from the design of the Heller mug. Massimo, thinking like an espresso-drinking Italian, designed the mug with a semi-circular opening at the juncture of the mug's rim and the trough-like handle. The mugs stacked into a sculptural form, with perfect circles defining the handles. It was a neat detail, easily appropriate with a small amount of espresso in a cup, but Americans typically drink big, full cups of coffee.

"Alan Heller contacted Lella and Massimo, saying there had repeatedly been complaints from the public and buyers about coffee coming out of that hole," said Luca. "Massimo, typically, was saying 'that is stupid customers who overfill their cups. If it has that design detail, then it should influence how they use the cup. They don't need instructions, it's right there—plainly visible—that you can't fill it all the way to the top.' Alan asked him to fill that hole. Massimo refused. It was a historic blow up, but finally he yielded to pressure when Lella said, 'come on let's do it.'"

"Lella's critical talent is her strong unabashed criticism. She is my brake, my reality, I could not have done this without her," said Massimo. While Lella cited recent times as her best years, Massimo decisively pointed back to 1964 and the insights he gained while working on the posters for Piccolo Teatro di Milano. The posters emerged through blending his understanding of architectural structure with respect for the work of Swiss graphic designers who were just beginning to influence the international approach to design. From that, his own vocabulary was established. It would form the basis of his entire career. "I focused on forms, elements—in effect, creating a catalogue of elements to use, so I wasn't starting from scratch all the time," he said. "Having a master language as a foundation is a very different attitude. There are people who just love to do the opposite, who can't stand this simple idea."

Massimo's vocabulary and his habits were well known by designers who worked with him. Yoshiki Waterhouse said, "Something beautiful just never grows old for him. For him, if it pleases him, that's all he needs—every time it is novel. I think that is unique. Most of us would get bored after a while, but Massimo sees everything with the eyes of a child. 'My God, look at this thing I have made!' It might be a letterhead, and he'll bring it and show it to us. And we will say, yes it is great, but it is the same one you do every time."[3] Massimo did not take shortcuts. Each solution went through his same meticulous process, even though his design team could often correctly anticipate where the final resolution would be.

The Vignellis agreed on a fundamental approach to their work, but continual questioning is what brought the work to completion. Lella was never afraid to question Massimo's decisions. As an example, she held up a cardboard model of a pitcher that was being designed for San Lorenzo. It was a cylindrical form, as Massimo had initially sketched. Lella was not satisfied. "I said no! They are looking for something new, something different—let's do something else." She proposed using a prism, a pentagon instead, with one edge creating a natural spout. Massimo drew it. She held up the second model, turning it to display its faceted form. It was clean, simple, but more visually assertive than the cylinder. "Then I thought, perhaps you could have another one, something new for summer, and it could be done with frosted glass and silver," she said. This blend of sensibilities, combining Massimo's sense of continuity with Lella's elegant adaptability is what makes the body of the Vignellis' work so balanced.

They consulted each other on most of their projects, large and small. The collaborative process was particularly helpful on showrooms and interiors that are created through a process of assembling many pieces, considering many aspects. The blend of their creative efforts distinguished this work. Caterina Roiatti said, "Lella was interested in taking care of the project: materials, the finishes, the production. She would go on-site and check colors, surfaces. She knew a lot about lighting. Both Lella and Massimo worked on refining details. They paid attention to the mechanical elements—ducts, sprinklers, for example—to either be not noticeable or to be deliberately presented. Their work is timeless, but it is of the time as well. They are always informed, always up to date, and the showrooms reflected the time; the art of the time in a way that was fresh, honest, straightforward."[4]

Showrooms attracted attention in the press because these spaces did much more than display a client's products. They were often notable design statements on their own. "It's hot, hot, hot and we don't mean the weather," wrote Edie Cohen for *Interior Design* in 1987. "The adjective refers to color— in supersaturated tropical shades—that forms the salient feature of the 1200-square-foot Artemide showroom design by Vignelli Associates. The vivid palette not only distinguishes the showroom from its predecessors, but also marks a departure for Massimo and Lella Vignelli, whose penchant for black/white/gray neutrals extends even to personal wardrobes. Apart from its distinctive color treatment, this most recent [Artemide showroom] follows a concept proven successful in their Los Angeles, Dallas, Houston, and Milan spaces, where product display is based on isolating so-called families of lighting, with each individual group shown in its own bay."[5]

The Vignellis have collaborated with Poltrona Frau since 1988, creating furniture and designing showrooms in Europe and in the United States. The Poltrona Frau showrooms were always among Lella's favored projects, and they too were positively received in the press. Jen Renzi wrote for *Interior Design* in 2003 about the opening of the Miami showroom: "The Italian manufacturer's colorful leather-upholstered furniture really pops in the design-district showroom, a coolly seductive space by Vignelli Associates." Renzi quoted Poltrona Frau's CEO, Giampiero Di Persia, "'It had to be a real Vignelli space, completely in their style,' he says. And it is. All clean lines and uncompromising vision, the functional and striking interior is scaled to display large collections and individual pieces equally well."[6]

Rather than managing a team of employees, the Vignellis now worked primarily with one or two designers. These relationships became even more intimate and familial. Lella developed new showrooms and interiors with architectural assistance from Paolo Leggi. While working with Benetton, Massimo met designer Piera Brunetta and in the typical interconnectedness of Vignelli relationships, she later came to New York to work directly with the Vignellis. For five years, Brunetta provided design assistance on every project, from books, wine labels, and packaging to a 2002 exhibition *The Italian Avant-garde in Car Design* which showcased thirty-two iconic cars at the New York Armory Building. Italian automotive manufacturers, including Pininfarina, were quick to promote the connection of being in the legendary setting of the "Armory Show" of 1913, the first large exhibition of modern European art in the United States.

For the Vignellis, work and life were always blended to be enjoyed. "It's not work, it's a way of being," said Massimo. There was more time to do so without the pressures of running a large office. This flexibility led to a new adventure in 2003, when they acquired a summer house in Nerano, Italy. The house, Casa Rosa, was perched on a cliff on the Amalfi Coast. They began spending two or three months there each summer. Massimo joked that Vignelli Associates actually had two offices: the winter office in New York, and the summer office in Italy. Their design staff moved with them and work continued as usual, with the welcome distractions of a beautiful view of the sea. "We rarely had vacations in our life," said Massimo. "Vacations are for people who hate work—definitely not my case! Most of our traveling was connected to work, lectures, conferences, and exhibitions."

Travel was part of intrinsic public relations for the Vignellis, although they would not use that term. They did not need to plan marketing campaigns, because promotion was a natural extension of their personalities, something they developed as students and built upon in all the years that followed.

Designer Graham Hanson worked with Massimo on the signage for Frank Gehry's Guggenheim Museum in Bilbao, Spain. Completing the project and attending the Museum's grand opening in 1997 provided Hanson with an opportunity to watch Massimo in action. "We had a blast at the opening. It was a grand affair. People from all over the world were there: designers, artists, architects, actors, press… Massimo knew them all. My wife and I stood on the balcony marveling at how Massimo worked the room with his magnetic personality, which he is known for second only to his design skills."[7]

The Vignelli personalities and their ease in creating connections came through in writing too. A continual flood of correspondence came through the office, and Lella wrote or oversaw most of it. No matter who was being addressed, even the shortest letters almost always included a personalized note within the message. Even if she was sending regrets, declining to participate in an event or donate to a cause, Lella found a way to convey that the recipient was special, noting something they did or said, something interesting in their project or positive in their life. She wrote many thank-you letters, praising a memorable event, congratulating a host, expressing appreciation for a meaningful gesture. These sorts of messages added to their reputations, maintained their connections, and helped to generate new and continuing business. Because Lella and the administrative staff were conscientious at keeping records, the Vignelli Archive is full of such correspondence.

While much of Lella's writing was based upon business correspondence, Massimo also enjoyed writing, particularly if he could address design issues. First in handwritten letters, later mostly through email, he willingly offered clarifying information about the world of design to colleagues, students, researchers, and writers from around the world. At times Lella tried to curtail some of this writing because of the amount of time he devoted to it, but she had little hope of stopping him.

After Brunetta returned to Italy, Beatriz Cifuentes returned to Vignelli Associates. She was a design intern in the Tenth Avenue office in 1999, and she was employed with other former Vignelli designers in the interim years. In 2008, Yoshiki Waterhouse returned to the office too, and Massimo often mentored a student intern, so the home office was a busy, but cozy, space.

Cifuentes and Waterhouse are, like Lella and Massimo, partners in work and in personal life. Working at Vignelli Associates changed with the times, but many aspects of work remained consistent.

Cifuentes said, "Sometimes I wonder how it was to work at the big office when Michael [Bierut] or Rocco [Piscatello] was there. It was much different than now. Our schedules are flexible; we may leave here at four, or at ten, and Massimo will say no big deal. In the office before, he traveled often and when he was in, a lot of people would want to speak with him. For us it is not like that." Waterhouse agreed. "We have unlimited access now. In that setting [Tenth Avenue] there were so many of us, we would work far more independently and only see Massimo from time to time. Being so close to Massimo is great, but as a designer one way to learn is by not having someone over your shoulder—doing a project by yourself, working out a lot of the kinks, and then showing him. That was the great thing about that time." [8]

In 2008, Beatriz was promoted to vice president of Vignelli Associates. Her work did not change, but the new title gave her greater status and authority with projects and clients. "Massimo is very clever from that point of view," said Cifuentes. "He's good at connecting with people and reading people; it is one of his traits along with his mastery of graphic design. He knows how people behave and react. When we go to meetings and travel—language is difficult. [Spanish is her first language.] I'm a very small person; I can be intimidated by having to make a presentation to the CEO. Massimo said, 'you need to be a vice president.' It made a difference for me, and for the clients it was different as well. He knows how to place people in the spot where he wants them to be. He knows how to prepare the stage to make things happen."

One of the projects that they worked on with Massimo was a renewal and expansion of the New York City transit map he originally created in 1972. While at Unimark, Massimo was instrumental in developing a signage system for the New York Metropolitan Transit Authority (MTA). That system has been effective and has been relatively unchanged in the decades since it was implemented. Later, he developed what became a controversial map for the system. Many users found it too diagrammatic, too lacking in geographic accuracy and representation. Their complaints were aggravated by the fact that it was poorly implemented; it was supposed to have been part of a mapping system, not a stand-alone artifact. Released in 1972, the map was mothballed after a few years, but conversation and debate about it never ceased.

The Vignelli design team revisited the 1972 map in 2008 after being contacted by *Men's Vogue* editor Mark Rozzo. Rozzo said, "I thought the project would be a great asset to our May design issue: a chance not only to cover design as a subject, but to be actually involved in creating great design with an acknowledged master. In a way, the project was also intended as a salute to Massimo himself at a time when so many people are again paying attention to the scope and enduring vitality of the work of Vignelli Associates."[9]

The revised map was inserted into the May 2008 issue of *Men's Vogue*. In addition, five hundred signed prints were sold, with proceeds given to Green Worker Cooperatives, a green business incubator in the South Bronx. Yoshi Waterhouse said the 2008 map was not a reconstruction of the original, but was newly built relying on current technology, including GPS and satellite images. "We used the pdf of MTA's bus maps as a reference because it has real vector artwork… they had all the stops in the correct geographic locations. That was actually a layer underneath our diagram."[10]

The story and evolution of the map has continued. Writing for the *New Yorker* in 2011, Paul Goldberger said, "Graphic designers turned it into something approaching an object of worship. In 2004, Michael Bierut of Pentagram wrote an eloquent homage to it, and in 2007 Gary Hustwit's documentary *Helvetica* spread knowledge of the map beyond design historians. An updated version of the map appeared in *Men's Vogue* in 2008. Nordstrom carried a Vignelli map dress, and Alexander Chen, a conductor (of music, not trains), turned it into an 'interactive string instrument.'"[11]

In 2011, the MTA introduced "The Weekender," a digital, interpretive version of the Vignelli subway map. This was also developed by the Vignelli team. This diagram (Massimo prefers to avoid the term "map") is thus far successful and functional since the diagrammatic approach provides clarity in the chaotic realm of the web and useful current information as an on-the-go app. Massimo said, "It doesn't make any sense to print a map anymore. In a digital era, a map should be a digital. The logic of a map is here, but the context has changed and all this information can come alive at any moment."

In 2013, researchers studying peripheral vision at MIT developed a computer model for assessing comprehension for at-a-glance map readers. *Fast Company* described the study in the Innovations in Design section with the subhead, "Massimo Vignelli really did know what he was doing." The research team in the Computer Science and Artificial Intelligence Laboratory generated a comparative study by altering maps, or as they said, creating "mongrel maps." The maps they studied, including the 1972 Vignelli diagrammatic map and the daily map that replaced it, allowed them to measure peripheral vision. These "sacrifice detail for overall impression to reduce the amount of data we process... So the mongrels effectively show what visual elements—color, text, space, line orientation, among them—have been condensed into pools during the map's journey from eye to brain... Looking at these mongrels is a way of confirming the designer's intuition."[12] Massimo has always insisted that information clarity is more important than geographic accuracy. Now science proves it.

On stage at the International Design Conference in Aspen, 1981.

Design Advocacy

Other designers may be as prolific as the Vignellis, but few are as completely engaged. Lella and Massimo continually added new roles and responsibilities to their schedules. Pride and pleasure in creating design solutions is only one aspect of their professional lives—they also feel an obligation to the world of design that demands their attention, criticism, and support. They have consistently worked to uplift and inspire the design profession from within; at the same time they have been visible and vocal at promoting societal advancement through design. This activism has been a defining attribute of the Vignellis since their student years at the University of Venice.

They have been active in many professional architecture and design organizations, Lella most often working behind the scenes, while Massimo held offices. He served terms as president of Alliance Graphique Internationale (AGI) and AIGA, and as vice president of the Architectural League of New York. They attend, often as presenters, national and international conferences and symposiums. They have been consultants to governments and business. They have served on juries and advisory boards, and offered critiques for industry, professionals, and students. Massimo nominated and endorsed fellow designers for professional awards and memberships. Separately and as a team, they amassed a staggering number of lectures, workshops, presentations, interviews, and exhibitions at venues around the world. Universities wanted their time: could they assist in identifying potentially visionary leaders for a school's design program? Would they be willing to visit campus and meet with students? Might a group of students come to visit their office? They said yes to these requests more than they said no.

In 1986, Lella was on the jury for the National Endowment for the Arts (NEA) Presidential Design Awards. That group, chaired by Lou Dorfsman, prepared a statement about standards for communications. Lella's attitude is evident in the statement's wording: "All design, government or private sector, should aspire to enhance its subject matter over and above merely reflecting it. The issue should not be the highlighting of individual items, but rather the overall improvement of standards..." Her input on design issues at a national level continued, as evidenced by correspondence with Donald Meeker. Meeker, whose firm specializes in graphic and environmental design, was working on the NEA Federal Graphics Improvement Program in 1989. He wrote to Lella saying, "I am not sure that there is enough understanding of what a federal design policy is, and I hope that the bureaucracy of the immediate past will not cloud the real issues when creating a future for this program." He asked for her assistance with "any ideas that might help shape this process." [1]

Massimo has contributed numerous articles to design journals. His approach in speaking and writing is often laced with humor, and he is not afraid of using attention-getting emotional outbursts to drive home a point. Lella was more verbal than literary, but at times she wrote descriptive and enlightening letters to clients. Her matter-of-fact approach provided them with insight into the breadth of a designer's thoughts on such issues as functionality, code compliance, cost effectiveness, and visual impact.

Lella was concise. Clients listened because of her logic. In one situation, she was advising a client whose existing office was literally and figuratively too noisy in both audio and visual ways. "Rethinking the materials of these areas is, in my opinion, a good chance to simplify an expensive and fussy solution." She also critiqued the client's office furniture, writing that one chair was "too small and delicate in construction," and other club chairs were "not appropriate, in my opinion, for the size of the office. They are too low in relation to their distance to the desk." [2]

The Vignellis are confident and articulate. People trust them and pay attention, though of course not everyone agrees with their approach. Only rarely were client relationships terminated. Often the threat of termination was enough to resolve an impasse. Designer Rocco Piscatello said, "Massimo would 'fire' clients who weren't meeting standards. He'd type a memo saying, 'You aren't seeing what we are seeing.' He would fax that memo and you could count on a phone call from the client twenty seconds later: 'We're so sorry!'" [3]

Piscatello said, "The Vignellis are from a generation when people didn't know what design was. Remember, we're talking about the 1950s and '60s, when the only people who needed graphic design services were corporations.

I think it is different now; clients today are more sophisticated," he said. A lot of the client interaction was explaining design: why we were doing things a certain way; what it meant to develop a design program; why consistency—with type, color, photography—was important. Never would we consider change for change's sake. When Massimo established a direction, people trusted it. Everything—every project—was done to the highest standards, or Vignelli Associates didn't do it. We were believers. No one doubted. When he set a condition, that was it—people were in awe of him."

Ivan Chermayeff, designer and lifelong Vignelli friend, understood how difficult client relationships could be, and how critical it was to communicate clearly in all ways, not just visually. "Tom [Geismar] and I were talking about this. In our own practice, in all these years, there haven't been more than ten or twelve clients who really understood what we were doing. You couldn't even say that you were a graphic designer at first; people did not know what that was." He suggested that educators needed to convey these issues to their students. "Now someone needs to make connections to different times, different cultures, and help students understand what design practice has been," he said. [4]

Chermayeff said, "Massimo is a consummate designer of order and cleanliness; very modern in spirit. I don't think of us as competitors, but as respected, trusted colleagues. His work is extremely consistent; one can see Massimo's work wherever it's applied and say, 'This is great, and it is typical Massimo.' The point is that sometimes it is more about Massimo's view of typography and the order of things than it is about the subject at hand, but the bottom line is that the Vignellis have been, and are, an extraordinary team. They support each other with genuine commitment and basic agreement every step of the way."

Discussion of design in America is often shallow, emphasizing "celebrities" rather than explaining or analyzing purpose, process, and meaning. Although Massimo enjoys some aspects of this—he certainly enjoys having "star" status—the limitations of this approach bother him. He has little patience for celebrity without substance, and serious concerns about the next generation of designers who are rising through this superficial atmosphere, lacking a foundation that, to him, is a fundamental basis for work and for life. Design education is often narrowly focused, funneling students into specific sorts of design practice with minimal insight into universal issues and opportunities.

"Designers are so specialized. Industrial designers do industrial things, a graphic designer does graphic design, a packaging designer does packaging—which is a lot of nonsense because a designer should do all that he can, and a good design company should be able to perform on all these levels in an interactive way. That's what we do—the whole spectrum," said Massimo. This attitude was natural to Lella and Massimo, instilled through education and experience from their earliest days as young Italian designers. It was part of what motivated them to leave Italy. They came to the United States and remained here because of the country's diversity, energy, and possibility, though they see the irony of being a land of wide opportunity that too often defaults to a narrow perception of design. Massimo said, "There is a greater need for design here; there are more things to fix."

While the Vignellis were often critical of missteps and missed opportunities in design, they were equally consistent in working to apply better design and to educate everyone in their path about why it mattered. In 1976, Massimo worked through the Federal Design Improvement Program, operated by the National Endowment for the Arts, to assist government designers in preparing better-printed materials. First in a seminar, then in a publication, he patiently explained the fundamental value of a grid, emphasizing its usefulness for workplace efficiency and for visual unity. He said, "A grid is nothing more than a tool. I know that particularly in this country, where people are not trained to use grids, there is a certain amount of fear about this tool and how to use it. It is much easier to arrive at a good, civilized, professional design with a grid than without a grid. It's a great thing!"[5] After that introduction, he carefully explained specifics of how to work with the tool, and issues to consider in developing it.

Sometimes Massimo felt like he was the only one who cared about these communication issues, but he did find some like-minded individuals and in 1977 he began an inspirational relationship with one of them, Vincent Gleason, chief of publications for the National Park Service (NPS). Vignelli Associates began working with Gleason and his staff to overhaul all of the NPS printed communications. More precisely, they worked to build a communications program out of the chaotic and inefficient flurry of more than 400 inconsistent publications and posters that were in use to promote the more than 350 separate National Park sites. Gleason had two primary concerns: reducing costs and creating a unified organizational image for the NPS. Considering that the NPS was printing and distributing approximately

20 to 25 million folders annually at the sites, and many of those titles had a life expectancy of ten to fifteen years, it was a major problem to solve.[6]

Gleason approached Massimo for the task after seeing the format he created for *The Herald,* in 1971. The weekly paper for the New York tri-state area folded within a year, but its pristine structure was unique and memorable compared to the loud and aggressive forms typical in the newspaper business. Gleason wrote, "The reason *The Herald* appealed grew from the fact that the NPS produces broadsides, many of which take the shape of a newspaper… I wanted a standardized format, much like a newspaper, with a basic design framework so that the staff could concentrate on content, not the evolution of clever layouts."[7]

To solve the problem of cost and to reduce waste, Massimo developed a "Unigrid System" that maximized efficiency for printing. He showed how this grid allowed ten different formats to be printed and cut from a single consistently sized sheet of paper. To bring distinctiveness and unity to the various NPS printed materials, he demonstrated how the grid provided an underlying structure to assist in placing photos, headlines, maps, and text into organized bands of information, no matter which size and format was being used.[8]

Vignelli Associates created the Unigrid System and training materials to assist NPS employees in learning how to use it effectively. An instructional broadsheet introduced the system, noting, "'Design'… is essentially the art and science of arranging the parts of an object, or of objects in a group, so that they serve the purpose for which the whole was designed and at the same time create seemly, harmonious, and beautiful entities. The Unigrid idea embraces this scheme of utility combined with beauty."[9]

The instructions described how park staffs and creative teams should work together. It explained the Unigrid's components, and how each functioned, noting, "A park folder is not a book, but a functioning site reference. It is much like a chart or map, to be opened as circumstances require." As a cost-saving measure, the system specified a single paper, purchased "…in carload lots for maximum discounts. This dull-coated stock takes both flat color and four-color reproduction. The paper offers rigidity, opacity, and toughness where map-folders will see rough usage over extended periods in possibly unfavorable weather. Its non-glare surface produces easy reading under bright skies—an important consideration at many NPS sites."[10]

Gleason said, "Massimo Vignelli sensed the magnitude of the problem from the start, envisioning a program with far wider public acceptance than had been possible with earlier random materials. At the outset of the redesign program, some staff designers viewed the planned standardization as too restrictive, believing it would curtail imaginative solutions. That attitude evaporated as the designers familiarized themselves with the principles and gained greater control over their work… One soon learns that the program's methodology is not as simple as it appears. The system calls for discipline and judgment every step of the way. Designers evolve effective solutions in direct proportion to the thinking applied to the job at hand. Far from inhibiting creative work, the Vignelli approach fosters innovation and careful workmanship." [11]

Massimo was recipient of the first Presidential Design Award in 1985, presented by President Ronald Reagan, for his work on the Unigrid and the NPS graphics program. "The award was special to me," said Massimo. "Winning that award validated my philosophy that design can improve our visual environment." Gleason agreed with that assessment, noting that Unigrid resulted in "useful guides for the traveling public." The NPS publications were popular in school classrooms, and handbooks were selling through park offices and the U.S. Government Printing Office.

Throughout his career, Massimo has been vocal about "fixing" design and his views have been widely disseminated. As early as 1968, speaking at the International Council of Graphic Design Associations (Icograda) Congress in Eindhoven, Netherlands, he was asked about the future of the design profession. During his speech, he noted, "If anyone would ask me where the design profession is going to be in the next ten years, or even where it is today, my answer would be it is 'in business.' Thank God we are moving away from the subjective, aesthetically oriented, fine arts approach which has been the basic structure of the graphic artists for the last eighty years or so. Now we are 'in business'… Our interest in the corporations or the community, the mass product and the mass communication media, is an interest which our profession has to share with sociologists, economists, planners, architects, etc. It is one of the aspects of the megastructure culture which we are going to face in the coming years, and it is the only direction we can take to make the social impact which is the ultimate relevance of our professional involvement." [12]

The Vignellis have not been alone in their condemnation of styling over substance; the topic has been discussed by many respected professionals. In 1983, industrial designer George Nelson wrote, "It is not a good thing for a designer to become a pimp… Creating new and unnecessary appetites for the marketing departments of the eternally hungry big corporations is not a dignified or even useful activity."[13] In 1995, graphic designer Paul Rand told his students, "Good design remains good no matter when it was done. [Good] design is universal and timeless… You do not worry about newness, you just worry about whether something is good or bad, not whether is it new. Who cares if it is new?"[14] Both these men fought against superficiality throughout their entire lives (Nelson died in 1986; Rand in 1996), but the issue remains for another generation to ponder.

In 1983, Rochester Institute of Technology (RIT) hosted The First Symposium on the History of Graphic Design: Coming of Age. The idea to place the Vignelli archives at RIT was borne during the planning for this symposium. Massimo was the keynote speaker. He talked about the need for study to understand of the *meaning* of graphic design, not just the *making* of graphic design. He challenged the audience to create livelier, more substantive design practice through raising standards of documentation, history, theory, and criticism. "As designers, we have to continuously sift the past and the present so that the things that remain on the top are the important ones, and the things that sift down are the gravel. We obviously want the golden nuggets at the top," he said. His summary statement: "If we don't make this step forward, we are all culturally dead, and if that is the case, Amen."[15]

The Fight against Ugliness

The Vignellis maintain a steadfast insistence on the validity of modernism, and their particular brand of it blends European tradition with American pragmatism. "The critics of modernism misunderstand. It is not a style issue, it is a moral issue," said Massimo. "It is imperative that design lasts a long time, as long as the material itself has integrity or until technical areas improve or change. Culture is important. Anything with value should be protected, whether it is a building, a package, or a bottle. These are the testimonials of a culture. Sometimes we protect things that are not timeless, but trendy; these are an expression of a particular time. We should not protect trash. People who understand this, who are critically motivated, should be making the decisions."

If they don't specify exactly who *should* be making design decisions, the Vignellis are clear that marketing personnel *should not* have this power. The topic always launches Massimo into an impassioned tirade. After leaving Vignelli Associates, designer Janice Carapellucci, remained in contact with her former employers. In 1994, she sent a letter, writing, "I miss you, Massimo, but you are with me every day. Thank you for preparing me so well… Did you catch this editorial blasting those marketing people?"[16] She attached a page from *The New York Times*. The headline shouted, "Marketers, Stop Your Tinkering," and the article offered a lively critique of the shortcomings of American marketing.

There is seemingly no end to this subject, or to the frustrations of seeing good design solutions bypassed or replaced for frivolous reasons. Paul Rand once wrote, "Persons unqualified to make design judgments are frequently shifted into design-sensitive positions. The position of authority is then used as evidence of expertise… At issue is not the right, or even the duty, to question, but the right to make design judgment. Such misuse of privilege is a disservice to management and counterproductive to good design." He concluded, "The plethora of bad design that we see all around us can probably be attributed as much to good salesmanship as to bad taste."[17]

Massimo has often said that a good design solution should be timeless; it should last until the problem changes. Unfortunately, that advice is often ignored. Good design solutions are often diminished by poor management and caretaking, or abandoned for reasons that have nothing to do with design value. Sometimes there is an uproar when this happens, but it can be difficult to know how much of the noise is critically motivated and how much is a result of a crowd-sourced mentality that presumes all responses have equal validity.

Design criticism is increasingly treated as a spectator sport, but architects and designers were condemning that practice long before current technologies made it easier to crowd out reasoned analysis through quick tweets and shallow messages. Just as design by committee rarely achieves concise solutions, critique arising from cacophony should be handled with caution. It has promoted poor design more than it has protected good work; the irony is that articulating this reality usually results in accusations of elitist design snobbery.

Sifting through all the noise allows one to pan for nuggets of enlightening critical commentary. In 2013 American Airlines announced a redesign that replaced the Vignelli identity program created in 1967. Critic Paul Goldberger condemned the new approach. He noted that the airline was in Chapter 11 bankruptcy proceedings. "So it's no wonder that somebody at American thought it would be a great idea to call up Future Brands—yes, that is the tellingly generic name of the design-and-consulting firm that came up with all of this—and ask them to give the airline a new image," he wrote. The company's management "somehow got the idea that the best way to deal with the struggles it has been having with its labor unions, its passengers, its rivals, and its investors was to change the way its planes look." [18]

Massimo said, "This is the typical mistake that company presidents make: 'I'll change the logo, and the company will look new and people will forget the company's problems.'" Public opinion has generally agreed that this change is not a good idea, with commentary about a "big waste of money by a company in bankruptcy" and observations that fixing the company image by "improving passenger experiences" would be a better place for management to focus its efforts. A cosmetic makeover is superficial styling—a use of design that the Vignellis abhor because it does not address inherent and important issues for the company and its clientele.

The Vignellis urge others to think carefully not only about what they are creating, but about how and why a solution arises. Massimo said, "There is a big difference between the people who ask why? and the people who say why not? *Why?* implies depth; people who ask 'why' are looking for structure, for what is good. To begin from *why not?* is a sign of chaos."

"We work through a process; it is the backbone of our methodology," said Massimo. "There is a process of thinking: examining, sifting, digging, exploring until you get down to the thing that is just right. It is very different from just finding something and saying 'How about this? How about that?' Sometimes you can do that; sometimes we *discover* by happenstance, but a lot of people get *seduced* by happenstance and that is a very different thing. That is the culture of the found object as opposed to the culture of the designed object."

Massimo continued, "Don't get me wrong. There are positive aspects even of the found object. You found it when your mind was focused on something; when you were thinking in a certain way. A thousand people went by that same thing and they didn't see it. It is not that it is a wrong way of working, it is a different way of working. Our way is more analytical; the other way is more happenstance. It takes a trained eye to see that happenstance and to see its value."

Massimo made the previous statement in 2006. It is consistent with comments he made years earlier. In 1993, he wrote a personal letter that challenged a leading American graphic designer, saying, "I see your sense of cultural responsibility being taken over by your desire to be different at any cost… In our culture and society, typographical refinement and design responsibility still have a long way to go. I know your intent is more noble than it looks and I respect it, but the form it takes is highly irresponsible since it breeds shallowness in the name of newness." [19]

The Vignellis are openly critical when others are less thorough or thoughtful. Not surprisingly, others are critical in return, railing against modernist minimalism as boring or predictable. Massimo cannot let such comments go unchallenged. "Is modernism static, fossilized—or is it dynamic?" he asks. "It is dynamic when you understand its essence!" Lella was also dismissive of criticism about their approach to their work. "There is always strong geometry in our designs. Geometry is not a fad, it is an eternal value. It lasts," she said.

Design historian Steven Heller wrote to Massimo in 1990, asking him to contribute an article for an upcoming issue of the *AIGA Journal*. He urged Massimo to describe his own ethic of design and its basis and foundation. "With insight into your own *raison d'être*, you will also be able to put into perspective the reasons for remaining true to a particular canon," Heller wrote, "I am interested in exploring design canon. The philosophical and ideological reasons why certain designers do what they do." [20] Heller correctly anticipated that Massimo would provide an impassioned response. It was published in the *AIGA Journal of Graphic Design* in 1991.

Massimo has consistently said that "Modernism is not a style. It is an attitude." His published response said, in part, "The ethics of Modernism, or I should say the ideology of Modernism, was an ideology of the fight, the ongoing battle to combat all the wrongs developed by industrialization during the last century. Modernism was a commitment against greed, commercialization, exploitation, vulgarization, cheapness… Much still has to be done to convince industry and government that design is an integral part of the production process and not a last-minute embellishment. The cultural energy of the Modern movement is still burning, fueling intellects against shallow trends, transitory values, superficial titillations brought forward by the media whose very existence depends on ephemera. Many of the current modes are created, supported and discarded by the very media that generates that change and documents it to survive. It is a vicious circle."[21]

A debate of old versus new and the clash of values and expectations was particularly spirited in the realm of graphic design and typography, especially as the profession was negotiating a technological shift to computers in the 1980s. The democratization of typesetting, for better and worse, spawned innovations that radically changed design. The resulting scramble for relevance was arguably the greatest change since Gutenberg's invention of movable type over five centuries earlier.

In his article, "The Obscene Typography Machine," published in *Print* in 1989, Philip Meggs tried to provide clarity and context for this new design world. Newly-empowered designers/typesetters often lacked awareness of the implications of their decisions, and Meggs tried to inform without alienating them. "Certainly, distortion can be a useful and innovative design tool when handled with sensitivity and intelligence, but we are seeing type distorted in violation of everything that has been learned over the past 500 years about making functional and beautiful letterforms,"[22] he wrote as he presented an introductory lesson on optical relationships within a typeface.

Either deliberately or through enthusiastic ignorance, with personal computers on their desks some people rejected rules of the past. Criticism rose from the eclectic explorations of this new generation of designers, creating what became known as post-modernism or New Wave. They were rebelling against reductivist visual form and reliance upon standards of structural organization. They were creating new and experimental typefaces, sometimes condemning the use of "old" types, Helvetica among them, in the process. This was, not surprisingly, heresy to Massimo.

Other designers were harshly dismissive of these new experimenters, unwilling to admit that a premise of exclusive design authority developed through years of experience was quickly evaporating. Massimo, like many seasoned designers, initially balked at this upset to his well-ordered world. Eventually he adapted and became more active in an educational role (if you can't beat them, then teach them), but until that happened, he was responsible for some lively discourse. He instigated an uproar by announcing that American designers use too many typefaces.

It started in 1991. The School of Visual Arts in New York selected Massimo as the recipient of its 1991 Masters Series Award (previous winners were Paul Rand and Milton Glaser). In conjunction with the award, Massimo developed an exhibition featuring five typefaces, because he was displeased with the distortions of form and the proliferation of what he saw as "junk" typography of that time. He intended to prove a point: that creativity did not rely on novel choices of typeface, but on thoughtful and appropriate applications of type. He noted that he was capable of doing most anything he needed to do by working with just five or six typefaces. Of course people wanted him to name them.

At various times, Massimo has named Bodoni, Helvetica, Garamond, Century, Times New Roman, (and if six, Futura) as the chosen typefaces. Rocco Piscatello thought about his experience at Vignelli Associates and said, "There's always been a huge controversy over the typefaces, and this is not a simple question. The modernists, Swiss graphic design—whatever you want to label it—have always believed in utilizing a limited type palette to ensure a consistent visual voice for the companies they were servicing. Simple, clear, and direct was the fresh water that the Vignellis were selling at the time. Massimo and I considered alternate typefaces and designed many projects using typefaces outside of the famous five. Massimo's bold and powerful approach to graphic design often clouds any memory of its typographic details. In the end, it is the form that we will remember most about the Vignellis' work, not the specific typefaces."[23]

Massimo's comments have generated lively conversations and passionate declarations of support or disdain for various typefaces ever since. Looking back at that time, he jokes about the uproar saying, "I was mad and I remember saying that I could cut the hands off those who manipulate and distort typefaces…. After that I received death threats." The comment about limiting typefaces has been repeated in other venues, including Massimo's book, *The Vignelli Canon*, but it is often disseminated without clarifying nuance: Massimo was specifically talking about readable typefaces for general text purposes. He is not the only one who advocates controlling the number of typefaces—many notable designers and design educators have said the same thing—but he is often more fun to hear.

Through both its content and its ever-varied visual form, *Emigré* (first published in 1984) became a leading graphic design forum for spirited discussion—and outright rants—in support of one side or the other as the digital age progressed. Editor Rudy VanderLans fueled the fire by challenging the opinions of, in his words, "the cranky old guys." On a positive note, these dialogues offered a starting point for developing more robust graphic design criticism and analysis, something that the Vignellis did support, but because *Emigré* was so visually exploratory in its form, that message was often obscured.

In the early 1990s, *Print* magazine sponsored a series of moderated debates that paired opposing design views. In 1991, protagonists Massimo Vignelli, type minimalist, and Ed Benguiat, who has designed hundreds of typefaces in his prolific career, surprisingly did not debate much. Instead they united in their distaste for *Emigré*. Massimo called it "garbage." "It deals with deformation as a thing to look for rather than to reject," he said. Benguiat said, "The only comment I have about *Emigré* is that when I look at it, I'm uncomfortable typographically. I think that readability, legibility is something people are overlooking." Both men like music, so Massimo used an analogy. "We like music and we can't stand noise. What we see here in *Emigré* is noise. Noise is a sound that has no intellectual depth," he said.[24] Ironically, a few years later, VanderLans changed the visual approach for *Emigré* to a cleaner, simpler format as he focused increasingly on criticism, analysis, and cultural context. Then it was the other side complaining because "the radical magazine was no longer radical."

Vignelli tirades against sloppiness, against superficiality, against post-modernism, became legendary. However, Massimo was just unpredictable enough to spur continued and lively interest. Although graphic designer Paula Scher was often disparaging of his beloved modernism and grids in general and Helvetica in particular, in 1988 Massimo endorsed her and Dan Friedman for membership in Alliance Graphique Internationale (AGI). Writing about Scher, he said, "Her use of typography is not mine, as you know, but it is one which I respect because it is meaningful and strong."[25] In 1992, Massimo again blasted *Emigré* as "A national calamity. An aberration of culture," although in 1996 he enthusiastically collaborated with the *Emigré's* founders, Zuzana Licko and VanderLans, even producing a poster to introduce Licko's typeface, Filosofia.

Massimo's poster offered an inside joke to those in the know as it proclaimed in large letters, "It's Their Bodoni." Filosofia was based upon Giambattista Bodoni's late eighteenth-century type design. The Vignelli office also had its own version of Bodoni (named Our Bodoni, drawn by Tom Carnese and released by Monotype in 1989). Designer Zuzana Licko wrote the descriptive copy for the poster. It included this statement: "Because Bodoni created so many variations, many different Bodoni revivals and interpretations are possible. However, determining which most truly reflect Bodoni's work can be eternally debated. Filosofia is my interpretation of a Bodoni. It shows my personal preference…"

Massimo didn't always rant. He could be poetic in expressing the mood of the day. In 1982, for example, he eloquently summed up three decades of design for U&lc magazine: "If the Sixties stressed the concept of discipline, and the Seventies that of appropriateness, the Eighties were finally intrigued by the pleasures of ambiguity." [26] Massimo's ability to craft succinct statements led his staff to coin the term "Massimo-isms," but the quick wit embedded in them was always grounded with meaning. That is what made them memorable.

In 2013, he wrote a poetic ode to his adopted New York City for Domus. New York is a place, he wrote, "where the door is open to everyone, where there are no ceilings, where everything is up to you and your energy, where if you are talented you will rise from your beginnings, where ambition is confirmed… where you experience a different kind of atmosphere and where there are no obstacles to vision. The city never stops changing. Retracing the same path several times in a month, you find new stores, new buildings, others that are restored. It is a city where the air you breathe is permeated with continuous action, presence, and absence. A city proud of its perpetual youth, aware of its own flux, fascinated with itself. This is the Vignellis' New York, a limitless city." [27] Ostensibly about the city, it could easily be an ode to their lives, successful and well-lived, as well.

Italian politician and journalist Furio Colombo wrote about Lella and Massimo in 1992. "Who are the Vignellis? I have known them for thirty years. Still the question is an appropriate one," he wrote. "Are they Italian, European, American? It is not a question of nationality. It is a question of cultural roots and cultural interpretation. Are they importing the past from the old country in order to create new things in the new world? If I am allowed to be a witness, I will state that I do not see the Vignellis traveling among and across different cultures in order to export and offer added value to what they do. The solid ground of their culture is with them, it is them." Colombo noted that their Italian and European history was integral, but, he said, "They are American the only way you can be one and make it in this country. By feeling intensely, exclusively yourself, creative, original, unique." [28]

Lella and Massimo have always lived life intensely, although with the passage of time they have less interest in being socially busy and a lessened ability to be so. Luca Vignelli said, "One of the reasons for their success is that working with them was not just about work. For the client, and for them, work had an entertainment value that was fun—and it was illuminating. People enjoyed working with them. They came away not only with problems solved, but they were more educated than when they first came into the office. They were now aware of aspects they would not have known before."

The Vignellis are not simply designers, they are also caring citizens, aware of and engaged in the world. A concern for cultural relevance and desire for the right to vote propelled the Vignellis into becoming American citizens. Massimo became a naturalized citizen on May 29, 2001. Lella made that decision much earlier, becoming a naturalized citizen on May 30, 1979. She was responding in part to an issue that concerned her from first-hand experience: the rising women's movement of the time, with calls for ending gender discrimination in the workplace. Valentina recalled that when she was young, she would hear other women complain about the limitations they faced, but in comparing those women to her mother, she was not impressed. She said, "At that point I was a teenager and I thought, why don't you stop complaining about it? Just go out and do it—like my mom."

Lella kept a folder in her office filled with articles about gender issues and leadership roles of female executives. During the 1980s and '90s she was busy not only with design, but with a wide range of social and cultural issues. She participated in planning sessions with the Cooper-Hewitt Museum. She was on the board of directors for the New York Landmarks Preservation Foundation. In 1985, she went to Charleston, South Carolina, to assist with reviewing plans for public housing. In 1988, she wrote letters to elected officials urging passage of a bill to fund research for Lyme disease. In 1989, she wrote letters about maintaining the integrity of a nature preserve in Sag Harbor (the Vignellis owned property nearby).

She got interested in politics, actively supporting Walter Mondale during his bid for the American presidency in 1984, in part because of his position regarding the roles of women and his selection of Geraldine Ferraro as his running mate. Through her position on the Steering Committee of Friends of the Arts for Mondale, she corresponded with Joan Mondale not only about fund-raising but about future planning and a role for design. She lobbied other notable members of the design and architecture community, including Milton Glaser and Bill Lacey (Cooper Union president), to assure their involvement as well.

In a July 1984 letter to Joan Mondale, Lella wrote, "I propose putting together a group of architects and designers so that we can concentrate on ideas related to these professions. And on the design issue, I propose creating a Design Council within the NEA [National Endowment for the Arts] (similar to the existing councils in England, Japan etc.). The aim is to make American Industry aware of the importance of design to beat the imported product competition from Europe and Japan. By Design I don't mean styling, cosmetics, or consumerism, but an economic tool to renew, streamline, and update production and products. American industry, from cars to appliances, has been suffering from elephantitis [sic] (pun on GOP) and the industry is too slow to change—so it falls behind the more dynamic approach of the Europeans and the Japanese."[29] Of course, Mondale did not win the presidency. Lella's engagement with politics was never as apparent afterward, nor is there evidence that government officials ever pursued her ideas.

Lella and Massimo were conscientious about supporting causes that they thought were worthwhile, sometimes through pro bono work at Vignelli Associates. They were active in professional organizations, and Massimo was a prolific writer too. For the most part, he focused on issues related to design. In 1992, Massimo wrote to Charles Orlebeki, an administrator at University of Illinois, because funding for the publication of *Design Issues* was in jeopardy. "*Design Issues* is one of the very few design journals in the world which is dedicated to history, theory and criticism," he wrote. "I understand that times are difficult, but it is in these situations that one can measure the relevance and courage of a humanistic university. In the ocean of communication, *Design Issues* has represented a beacon of intellectual stimulation and cultural depth that cannot be turned off without leaving us in the darkness of ignorance."[30] Whether his letter made a difference is hard to say, but at least he tried; that university ceased support for the journal in 1993, but it is still published by MIT Press.

They were unrelenting in their attempts to enlighten others about the power and purpose of design. Lella said, "As architects we are responsible for people's microenvironment, the things that surround us on a daily basis. Both of us feel strongly about the notion of timelessness. We feel a responsibility toward the client; we hate trendiness and ephemeral things."[31] She continued, saying, "In design of household objects and furniture there is no room for trends, it's not a throw-away thing. If you get a new chair, you want to keep it for the rest of your life. You live year after year with what you buy. So we try to create things that will last forever."[32]

Massimo said, "We do not have a style, but we do have an attitude. An attitude is a state of mind, and for us it is very primary. We try to be strong, clean, and to the point with everything that we do." Design is different from styling, though every object has elements of both. The Vignellis are confident in their commitment to one and consistent in their condemnation of the other. Massimo gets riled just thinking about it. "In America, styling prevails over design, and that tragedy is spreading around the world. Now, instead of spending energy making good things, designers have to spend energy fighting this problem. It is like the resistance against a dictator!" he says. "We underestimated the American love of novelty. That is based on the notion of obsolescence and it is simply a stance for making money."

In 2013, Robert Swinehart, emeritus professor at Carnegie Mellon School of Design, said, "The modernist idea of longevity, of developing work with lasting meaning, is undergoing a struggle. People don't take the time to know their values, to know how values are expressed through the product and for the client. Because of technology, things happen quickly. If design, as a body of information, isn't strong enough to hold up in use, it shouldn't be around, but the timeframe now seems to be week to week, even minute to minute. Why talk about depth and lasting impact? Unfortunately, that idea gets dismissed as outdated."[33]

"We have always worked to spread the gospel of good design," said Massimo. "We describe our work as democratic—it is giving people what they *need,* not what they *want.* It is a healthy notion of democracy, not a corrupted notion of democracy and freedom. Freedom is not a license to do whatever you want. That is not freedom; that is just the opposite. It is anarchy."

Massimo critiques the work of Michael Gagliano and Marco Zannini, who traveled from Milan to attend the Master Designer Workshop at the Vignelli Center, July 2013.

Students, Teaching, and Learning

The time for tirades has mostly passed to be replaced by the time for teaching. In *The Vignelli Canon,* Massimo writes, "Creativity needs the support of knowledge to be able to perform at its best... With great pleasure, I look back to all the moments when I learned something new in typography, either from a master or from fellow practitioners... that beautiful feeling of enrichment that comes from new new discoveries, new ways of doing the same thing better than before." [1] Massimo and Lella are sharing their knowledge with a new generation of designers and scholars. The world holds much for students to learn and now the Vignellis are focused on the students, on the learning, and on the future.

Examining the work of their lifetime is one thing; considering Massimo and Lella when they were students themselves is just as illuminating. Lella was an excellent student who chose an appropriate path from the start and followed it consistently. Massimo struggled, but persevered, growing through a combination of formal education and individual initiative. Ultimately a traditional educational path was not right for him, but he became a learned man and he has never stopped encouraging others to learn.

The Vignellis remember those times and it gives them empathy though not necessarily great patience—they are very clear about the consequences of choices. Being successful starts with being disciplined. "When you are a student, you have choices," said Massimo. "Do you want to go skiing with your friends, or do you want to learn and be involved in design for changing society, improving quality of life? The only way to emerge from the crowd is through passion and enthusiasm. This hasn't changed. The good students tend to congregate and stick together and become the promoters of the professions, but ninety-nine percent of students are there simply to get a job. We were there to be leaders of the profession. It is a choice."

"I know that teaching can elevate those without talent, but I think it may be better to educate those with talent so they can grow and produce something of significance. When I see a student with passion, I treasure them; take good care of them." said Massimo. He has been particularly generous in writing back to students who contact him directly, often sending long handwritten letters (or later, emails) to critique, inspire, and encourage. He unfailingly tells them to read, to study, to think about and analyze design history, theory, and criticism. He remembers that star-struck feeling of meeting his heroes. Now Lella and Massimo are the heroes, and the young people are often shy, a bit intimidated, but excited by any opportunity for conversation, for connection. It shows in their smiles, in their attentive listening, in their excitement.

"Dear Mr. Vignelli," introduces sincere letters arriving from students all over the world. They wanted his advice, they wanted his critique, they sometimes just wanted to say that he inspired them. An architecture student in Canada wrote to ask what books he should read, what practices he should follow. A design student in Wisconsin wrote to learn more about the early years of Vignelli practice. Through Massimo's thoughtful responses, he has surely inspired them even more.

A design student in Scotland developed a "Vignelli retreat" as a class project. She also furnished the space and wrote a long letter to describe it. "Perhaps you wouldn't approve of me adapting your original ideas to complement my design, but I felt if you were to design this retreat, you would design everything from the cutlery to the bed linen, so it didn't seem right to fill my design with unknown furniture," she wrote. [2] Massimo's two-page response was both personal and insightful. "You should know Scotland holds a very dear place in my heart because I took my wife, Lella, for a honeymoon in Scotland to see all the great works of Adams and MacIntosh [sic]," [3] he wrote. Then he discussed her project. "One of the things that impresses me most about your project is your ability to understand your clients, down to the last detail. This implies a tremendous sense of observation, even more so since you have never met them." Massimo provided an in-depth critique of her solution, agreeing with many aspects and critically dissecting others, adding suggestions for improvement. He encouraged her to keep learning, keep in touch, and to come visit should she ever be in New York. "All the best wishes for you and your work. Again, many thanks for gracing us with your beautiful project," [4] he wrote, the letter ending with the flourish of his distinctive signature.

Lella also reached out to students, visiting countless schools for studio critiques. "I enjoy working with young people," Lella said. "I think that I can put together information well. I can explain what they can do; what has value.

Sometimes they need help in knowing what to do: trying different things, or using materials in a different way. Sometimes they stop before they should—some people try a range of things, but others limit themselves. Designers are doing so many different things now; the young designers should try to do that too. They see new things, new designs, they know what other people are doing, they see what is coming out."

In the classroom as in the office, Lella is consistent; she works through a process of critique and analysis. It is more verbal than visual. "When I work with the students I look at what they do and what is important—what should stay and perhaps what can be changed. What is beautiful, what they should forget." Valentina was listening to this conversation. She laughed and said, "And what she would say? She would say, 'It's too much!' She is not much for subtlety." Lella agreed, "I do say it's too much. I have figured things out for myself and now I can share it with them."

Lella brings a different perspective to her engagement with students. She remembers times when others thought gender should limit her potential. She shares the realities that she faced in being a designer plus having the responsibility of running the office. "I tell them that women can have problems because they are women. Sometimes I would threaten to leave the office, but of course I couldn't. Most men do one thing at a time, but not women!" she laughed. "I do not want to work like a man—unless they are really very good—but men have the attitude that they can do things just because they are men. Men are men; even in class the boys listen differently. When something has value for the men, often they get more involved—learning things like fabrication, for instance. I can explain that fabrication is important *for everyone*."

"For the young women, I bring integration. They ask me questions; the girls are paying close attention to me," Lella said. "Often they are sitting in the back and I go to them and say, 'I am speaking to you now.' I tell them be assertive… don't be afraid to come out in discussions with your own point of view, don't be afraid to be heard. You must have faith in yourself, in your ideas, because there are enough other forces trying to keep you down." Lella urges all the students to read. "Look for examples, read biographies… It's very important to be able to compare your situation with other situations. This is especially important when you are just getting started and you don't yet have the range of experience to help you through some of the situations you might encounter."[5]

If students focus on the glamour of the Vignellis, they are quickly grounded by some very practical information. The Vignellis teach in part by setting an example. They talk about choices and about setting standards. Massimo advises students, saying, "You cannot build the future if you don't have an awareness of the past and a knowledge of the present. Learn about issues and ideas which have provoked change."

They talk about doing good work. What is a "bad" client? "A bad client doesn't understand the role of the designer," says Massimo. "Designers are like doctors. You don't go to the doctor and tell him what you *want*—you ask the doctor to give you what you *need*. It should be the same with design." What does it mean to have integrity? They share experiences to help students understand that sometimes it is better to walk away than to compromise.

One example happened years ago, but the lesson is timeless. Massimo was commissioned to design a poster to be part of an American Bicentennial series in 1976. As an immigrant, he chose to focus on the theme of "the melting pot." Buying every foreign-language newspaper that he could find in New York City, he used segments of them to create an American flag. Though the idea was accepted, one bureaucrat in Washington, D.C., wanted him to recreate the poster "with better news." Whitewashing or faking facts would have undermined the integrity and the pluralistic point of his message, but standing up for his point of view meant that they wouldn't print it. Massimo refused to alter the design. He never had much patience for bureaucrats or approval committees, and this experience cemented his distaste for political maneuvering, no matter what the group might be. The poster was privately printed as a limited-edition silkscreen, but it was not disseminated as part of the Bicentennial series.

Massimo said, "It is useful to convey the importance of lifestyle to students— how important elements of lifestyle can be—but it is important to remind them how that glamour was achieved. It was not by independent means or preposterous fees. It came through a lot of work at standard professional fees. Connections are extremely important; from one project, another takes place. Honest interest and genuine enthusiasm are great ingredients for obtaining new projects, new challenges. We tell them that you have to decide what is more important in your life: making money, or making a statement. If it is making money, design is probably not the way to reach that goal. But if you are interested in improving society, design is a very good tool."

The Vignelli Center for Design Studies

When Rochester Institute of Technology (RIT) hosted a graphic design history symposium in 1983, it was a first step in a bigger idea for design and for the university's advocacy of it. Since that time, the university, primarily through the efforts of Professor R. Roger Remington, has been collecting archives of modernist graphic designers. As of 2013, thirty-five archival collections already exist on campus, and more have been promised. Remington (now the Vignelli Distinguished Professor of Design) and the Vignellis spoke often about the growing collection and discussed the potential of adding their body of work to RIT. It took twenty-seven years to make that happen.

Lella and Massimo designed a new building. Golden shovels in hand, they broke ground for it at a ceremony in October 2008. The exterior appears to be two cubes, one of glass tucked into another of brick. The glass cube presents two floors of exhibitions, with part of the space permanently arranged to display examples of Vignelli works and a flexible open area to feature traveling exhibits, lectures, and public events. A third floor at the top offers a more intimate meeting and study room; this has been the scene for summer workshops and for meetings with studio classes during the academic year. The actual archives fill much of the brick cube. Work is ongoing to catalogue the vast quantity of papers, sketches, models, and final products held within.

Other institutions were interested in attaining the Vignelli archives, but Lella and Massimo liked the attitude and the hands-on access at RIT. Massimo said, "RIT is a living teaching institution and that is the difference—they actually use their archives; it is a living tool. It is not in the basement or an attic. The students use it. Roger Remington showed vision, courage, and determination in making this dream a reality. The Vignelli Center is not only the building and the archives, but it is sharing our philosophy of the importance of design theory, history, and criticism. That is RIT's philosophy too."

The Vignelli Center for Design Studies at RIT officially opened with a three-day dedication ceremony in September 2010. It was a major design event as about five hundred visitors came from around the world to share the excitement and to honor the Vignellis. The RIT campus was awash with guests, sometimes generating some puzzled looks from campus regulars. (It was a design event, so not surprisingly, the predominant wardrobe color was black.) After years of thinking and planning, after the turmoil of construction and the organization of truckloads of artifacts, finally the Vignellis were inside of "their" building, surrounded by an approving crowd of well-wishers.

The occasion was festive, but not without tears. More than once Massimo wiped tears of happiness, while Lella, usually the more stoic of the two, lit up the space with a beaming smile. They lined up with the university president, Dr. William Destler, and Lady Helen Hamlyn to cut the ceremonial ribbon. The support of the Helen Hamlyn Trust of Great Britain was critical to funding the construction of the Vignelli Center and it provides ongoing support for the Massimo and Lella Vignelli Distinguished Professor of Design. The main exhibit gallery in the Vignelli Center, the Benetton Gallery, is named in honor of a major donation from the Benetton Group.

In recognition of his efforts in bringing the Vignellis to RIT and establishing the Vignelli Center for Design Studies, R. Roger Remington was selected as the first person to fill the endowed professorship. Remington said, "Through the scope and integrity of their work, the Vignellis have influenced design for more than four decades. Massimo and Lella have been the champions of modernism, and it is our responsibility through the Vignelli Center to extend that legacy. I agree with their thoughts that modernism is enduring and timeless. Massimo has been very clear about this. It is instructive for people to hear his position, and it is important that students have exposure to this—in studio and in history—and then they can decide where they fit. Massimo and Lella have invested their lives in the belief that design is both a lens through which to view the world and a useful tool in building better futures. Their work is more than functional product, and the Vignelli Center for Design Studies is far more than a building. It is design classes and student portfolio reviews; it is generations of design students who will benefit from exposure to the principles of good design. It will be a destination for students, faculty, designers, and scholars from around the world."[6]

The Vignelli archives now reside alongside those of design pioneers Lester Beall, Will Burtin, William Golden, Alvin Lustig, Cipe Pineles, and many others. The cumulative effect of all these original materials brings context to all the work. To understand the progression of American design, "you need time, you need perspective," said Massimo. "The only time you get the proper perspective is after seeing both the impact of your work and historically what role it played. The archives—where students can see the whole thing, from sketches and models to final pieces—there is nothing comparable, no photo that can compare to handling and working with the real thing."

Visiting Rochester, New York during construction of the Vignelli Center for Design Studies, June 2010.

Massimo working at home with Beatriz Cifuentes and Yoshiki Waterhouse, 2011.

A Lifetime, and No Regrets

A lifetime of effective design solutions, diverse clients, professional visibility, and international recognition has provided real satisfaction, but now the Vignellis face inevitable changes and endings. Here too they have been systematic. They've successfully launched the Vignelli Center for Design Studies, and they have had the satisfaction of lecturing and teaching in the space. They have seen it come alive with learning. The continuing legacy of the Vignelli Center is likely to become their most important work.

Professor Robert Swinehart said, "As professionals, the Vignellis have achieved one of the highest levels of success because they held onto the highest ideals. They have been extremely consistent even though they have designed just about anything that can be designed. Their work has strength. It is so useful, so simple, that it is almost nude. Some would say 'simplistic,' but their work rises above the criticism because they embed a philosophy and functionality that drives their thinking and puts it on a higher plane. Time has validated them with name recognition that spans the globe."[1]

Designer George Lois joined Massimo at the Vignelli Center for a workshop in 2012. "Massimo loves the students; he sits with each student and spends hours with them. He's tough with them, but what a thrill it is to get that very specific attention. He started at 8:00 a.m. and he was still going strong at 8:00 p.m." said Lois. "While we were in Rochester, I was working on my book and he was curious about it. I showed him Lesson 118: *If you do it right, it will live forever.* Now Massimo uses that line with me; he brings it up every time we are together. That is what Massimo and Lella have been about all their lives: doing it right. Because of the Vignelli Center, their attitude will live forever."[2]

During its summer workshops, the Vignelli Center comes alive. For four years, Massimo and Lella conducted master design workshops in France, working with fellow designer and longtime friend Armando Milani. The location, at the summer home of Armando and his wife Cynthia, brought designers together from across the globe, giving them a taste of beautiful

Provence as well. In 2010, Ashraf Elfiky flew from Kuwait to attend. "You have no idea how much the workshop in France was useful to me. It was as if I was living in a different world and suddenly my eyes opened on a different dimension to what I do,"[3] he said.

While Rochester, New York doesn't offer quite the same level of tourist appeal as Provence, France, the excitement of attending workshops at the Vignelli Center has been just as strong, the results just as enlightening. Students who attend have a hunger for learning, for critique, and the workshops provide a substantial dose of both. Lasting relationships arise from the workshop experience. Many attendees continue to have regular contact through social media, sharing advice and their ongoing enthusiasm for the world of design. Several attendees are workshop veterans, who return again and again to work with Massimo and RIT designers.

Sean Wolcott, a mostly self-taught designer from Snohomish, Washington, is one of them. "When I saw the *Vignelli Canon* in 2007, it changed my life by making things crystal clear," Wolcott said. "Then I was listening to interviews with Massimo and had an impulsive thought that I would like to meet him in person. That's when I discovered the Vignelli Workshop. After working with Massimo first-hand, making decisions, listening to his recommendations, talking about 'why,' there has been a noticeable change in my work, and when I returned the next year, he recognized and complimented my growth. My biggest take-away from these experiences is that good design is a language. There is good and bad—it is not dogmatic; there's a clear rationale. It's teachable and it is a tool for reaching others."[4]

In 2013, Michael Gagliano, a design student at Istituto Europeo di Design (IED) in Milan, attended the Vignelli Workshop for the first time. "I found out about Massimo during my first year of university. I found the *Vignelli Canon* online and started reading more, watching videos—he became my mentor, and I wanted to be like him. I actually found out about the workshop last year, but I had to save money for a year to be able to come," Gagliano said. "This has been an opportunity to look at design from a different perspective, and I now see myself in a new way—I will never work the same way again. My dream job is opening my own firm, a good firm. I don't want to compromise that vision; I would like to reach Massimo's age and be regarded, like him, as someone who has accomplished something important."[5]

The students want to learn about grids and how to use them. They often complain that their education was lacking in this area of learning and they listen attentively as Massimo shows and explains how to develop and work with a grid. This is a presentation that Massimo knows intimately, having made it in his earliest days in the United States helping Unimark designers; in the 1970s and '80s working with non-profits and federal agencies; and into the twenty-first century working with workshop students. It saddens him that many educational institutions haven't done better in conveying this critical and useful information. It validates his efforts with the Vignelli Center, and it pleases him that, year after year, the students want to learn.

The seventeen attendees at the 2013 Vignelli Master Designer Workshop came from Ecuador, Germany, Italy, Mexico, Puerto Rico, and from across the United States. Some were already practicing designers, while others were students. One had a special connection to Massimo: his granddaughter, Maya Zimmer. She attended the workshop for a second year. Now completing her final year of high school, Zimmer is making plans to study graphic design. Although she hasn't chosen her university yet, flying from Germany to study with her grandfather has given her a good foundation. Of course Massimo is pleased about this. "To have Maya interested in graphic design makes me very, very happy," he said. "To see her progress without any training is spectacular, and I am very pleased with the results of her project. I think she has a natural talent. Knowledge will follow as her interest gets deeper… I hope she will continue to be a designer with an independent intellectual life—just as Lella has done."

The search for meaning and understanding has been a constant aspect of the Vignelli design process, but now there are new experiences to face. It is hard because the Vignellis seemed to be unstoppable, but recently that began to change. In December 2009, Massimo flew to Chicago for the release of the *Unimark International* book. Before he left, Lella was worrying about him. "Make sure he wears his hat and gloves, keep an eye on him," she fussed. By the time the plane landed, he had received multiple phone messages as Lella and Beatriz Cifuentes were both calling. "I felt like I had two wives," Massimo grumbled good-naturedly as he returned their calls.

Lella seemed forgetful, anxious, and increasingly distracted. Medical tests confirmed a diagnosis of Alzheimer's dementia in fall 2010. As is typical of the disease, onset was gradual and fluctuating; at times everything seemed normal. She began organizing her work, straightening her records. Caterina Roiatti said, "Lella's problems first became noticeable in paying bills. She was confused and asked Luca for help; it became too much for her. When she got sick, Massimo stepped up. He began asking me questions: what to do when employees are sick, how much to pay…"[6]

At the beginning of their career in 1966, Lella and Massimo left Milan to come to New York. They were excited about the new opportunity, but little things—things they never expected—were hard. "You feel homesick. You have left your friends, you are in a new place, even food is different," said Massimo. "There are cultural differences; silly things you learn in early years without even realizing it, like a song which has a lot of meaning for many people because they grew up with it. Or a word, or a poem, or a person, an actor—I didn't have the context, I didn't know the rules. Some of the people you work with accept that, some are amused by it; others are irritated." Eventually, if you are observant and thoughtful, the new becomes familiar. Now near the end of their careers, they are entering another new and unfamiliar phase.

Several years ago, Massimo was contacted by a fan who caught his interest by asking a question, will mankind survive the century? Massimo responded, noting that awareness of issues—political, environmental, or otherwise—was the first step toward resolving them. "A fundamental trust in mankind is the necessary attitude to prevent things from happening." he wrote, describing various ways that people were addressing problems to create a better world, a bright future. He noted his overall positive attitude toward the future, although he admitted, "sometimes the blues may take over temporarily."[7]

One of the things that makes Massimo a pleasure to be around is that sunny attitude. Lella's illness makes it difficult, but Massimo's characteristically upbeat outlook and good humor usually prevails. He says that they are simply exploring new terrain. The home office, once simply a convenience, is now a necessity. "It is very important for Lella to have her own office, where she is comfortable and pretends to be busy. She is still surrounded by books related to her work. We will stay here until the last day of our lives; particularly for Lella it is important to live in a familiar environment," Massimo said.

He has gained new understanding of all that Lella managed for their lives and careers. "I want people to recognize her as an intelligent and beautiful person, a professional and constructive partner. There has never been one second in my life that I had a doubt about those qualities," said Massimo. "I see Lella as one of the great Dames of Design, who was doing things without any fanfare; doing them right because there are no alternatives to what is right."

Most of the time, Beatriz Cifuentes and Yoshiki Waterhouse work from their own home office now. They continue to collaborate with Massimo on architectural books and other projects, but this arrangement is simpler for everyone. "They have adopted us; it's like we are their son and daughter," said Waterhouse. "It shows in so many ways—there is such a tenderness. I would never have that in another employer relationship; it's comfortable, very generous, and open—and Italian. Massimo has the same dealings with his clients too, he develops extremely personal relationships so they are all close friends."[8]

Cifuentes agreed. "That was almost the rule. I think it's because of the way Massimo treats people—it is that approachability. Even when he meets new clients, he has this family attitude; they become good friends, they go to dinner together—maybe it's cultural? The clients relax, and it also applies to the people that work with them. They consider us part of the family and we consider them to be our family."[9]

Alan Heller has been one of those client-friends for decades. "I started a small housewares company, and I went to Italy to see what I could find. I picked up *Domus* and *Abitare* and couldn't believe it—the stuff was nothing like we'd seen in New York. I wanted something like this! Friends said, talk to the Vignellis. So I did. I have known Massimo and Lella since 1967 and we have been working together ever since. Our connections are emotional. They have been mentors to me, and through them, I was seduced by the Italian culture. They are charming and delightful; Lella is solid and grounded— and sensual. Massimo at times is an exploring four-year-old. Out of that combination comes unparalleled creativity. Absolutely everything we've ever done is as fresh today as when it was done. It is practical, appropriate, and timeless. To do something exquisitely doesn't necessarily cost more. They have extraordinary vision and we have the perfect relationship of designer, product, and client."[10]

"The Vignellis have meant so much to us in terms of our life," said Giorgio Spanu. "There is such integrity in everything that Massimo does; he has taught me to live this same way."[11] Long after the collaboration on their Murano Glass exhibition and book finished, the relationship with the Vignellis continued. Nancy Olnick agreed with her husband. She said, "They are two extraordinary people with great synergy between them. They have such a good fit, a good marriage; they inspired us in our relationship. Lella was helpful to me in ways apart from work; as a woman, wife, mother; she has been caring, listening, and supportive. I admire her so much in how she's lived her life. Her thinking was so crystal clear; knowing about the dementia makes it hard for me to talk about this now… She was one of the smartest, most decisive women I've ever met." [12]

Beginning in 2001, Lella and Massimo created an extensive range of work for the Feudi di San Gregorio winery near Naples. Owner Antonio Capaldo said, "Massimo and Lella quite extensively showed not only their talent and creativity, but also their capability to be distinctive in a broad range of possible applications. They designed the whole identity: logo and brand communication, the labels, the stands for wine fairs, the interior of the winery, a wine bar we own near Naples, brochures and many other things." [13] Massimo designed a book about the winery; Luca contributed many of the photographs in the book.

The warmth in their relationship with Capaldo is predictable. In 2013, Capaldo said, "I personally started working with Lella and Massimo in 2009, and the first thing that impressed me was the youthfulness of their minds. Between me, now thirty-six years old, and Massimo—he is the younger, the braver, the more visionary." Capaldo said, "…Everything is expressed by his trilogy: vision, courage, and determination. The vision needs to remain clear and stable but an entrepreneur needs to have courage to explore new ways and determined to try, and try again. Lella has always been his perfect match, managing some of his extremes and applying a reality filter to some of his dreams."

Capaldo said, "Massimo is one of my greatest mentors. I try to follow his lessons in my professional life. One thing that impresses me about Massimo is that he listens. He is a superstar designer, he is now more than eighty, and yet he listens to his clients very carefully. This does not happen so often—I work also with other designers/architects and I can tell. It will sound a bit silly and simplistic, but I think they found the perfect way to put together the Italian creativity and color with the American structure and pragmatism. They make timeless design in an elegant way. I think that the wine labels are most meaningful: iconic, unique, innovative—they make our image still distinctive, modern, and elegant ten years after we adopted them."

"Today I am standing with great serenity because of my values and discipline," Massimo said recently. He talks about intellectual elegance. "People need to realize that integrity is the essence: in a moral sense; in design; in lifestyle, clothing, language. Profanity is everywhere," he said. "People say, 'I talk like this with my friends, but not in public.' Why have a dichotomy like that? Can't you express yourself in a better way? How can you expect to design elegance if you are talking like that? There needs to be truth to principles, with inner integrity as an innate part of being, not as a convenience."

Massimo has often been quoted about his reverence for an orderly life. "Everything has its own order. You can't take a piece of music and scramble the notes. You can't take a piece of writing and scramble the words. You can't take a space and scramble the chairs around,"[14] he said. It has not been easy to adjust to Lella's illness. He misses the order and the critique that she added to their partnership, but after a lifetime together her voice is not lost to him. "Now I perceive her in a symbiotic way so she can still play a part in my work." Assisting with her care is now part of his work as well.

"Timing is the essence, luck and timing. Today we'd be a drop in the ocean, we would disappear. But at the time we began, very few had the drive, the discipline, the knowledge," said Massimo. "We came to the United States because there was a need for us to be here. To do something well, to do it badly—it costs the same. We thought we could help with design by showing better alternatives, by offering a different visual language and teaching people to use it. We have tried to teach people that good design is a good investment."

Massimo looked at Lella and smiled. He said, "We have had the delight of working in the intimate scale of the home surroundings at the beginning and the end of our professional life. We had the satisfaction of a large and gorgeous office—a tangible manifestation of our own style and personality— that signaled the professional relevance of our work. I am glad to have had both in great measure. Looking back, NO REGRETS!!!"

Notes

The Vignellis: An Introduction

1   The Architectural League NY, "President's Medal 2011: Massimo and Lella Vignelli, archleague.org/2011/03/presidents-medal-2011-lella-and-massimo-vignelli/ (accessed August 7, 2013).

2   Massimo Vignelli, *Lella and Massimo Vignelli: Design Is One* (Victoria: The Images Publishing Group, 2004), p. 4.

3   RIT, *The University Magazine,* "Vignelli Center, Opening in September, Has Worldwide Connections," Kelly Downs, www.rit.edu/news/umag/fall2010/5_vignelli.php (accessed June 15, 2013).

Foundation: Growing Up in Italy

1   Melissa Seiler and Pat Kirkham, "Lella Vignelli on Vignelli: Design History, Concepts,
    and Collaboration," *Studies in the Decorative Arts* (Fall/Winter 2000), p. 139.

2   Robert Traboscia, interview, January 17, 2013.

3   Deyan Sudjic notes that Rogers wrote something very much like it in a 1952 editorial for Domus. Sudjic, *The Language of Things: Understanding the World of Desirable Objects* (New York: W. W. Norton, 2009), p. 34.
    Researching this question shows the danger of assuming that information on the Internet is correct. Several sites attributed the quote "spoon to a city" to architect Argo Flores. Argo Flores does not exist! A poor transcription of a video interview with Massimo is the starting point for the fictitious Flores: someone misunderstood Massimo's accent and didn't know enough about architecture to check on the name. Other links to the same transcription have spread this inaccuracy across the Internet.

4   David McFadden, "Design Comment: An Interview with Lella Vignelli," *Glass Art Society Journal* (1986), p. 30.

5   Gino Moliterno, ed., *Encyclopedia of Contemporary Italian Culture* (London: Routledge, 2000), p. 33.

6   Caterina Rioatti, interview, February 2, 2013.

7   Ibid.

8   Seiler and Kirkham, "Lella Vignelli on Vignelli," p. 141.

9   Ibid., p. 142

1965: Unimark International

1   For further information about Unimark, read Jan Conradi, *Unimark International: The Design of Business and the Business of Design* (Zürich: Lars Müller Publishers, 2010).

2   Robert Craig, interview, November 7, 2006.

3   Franco Gaffuri, interview, June 15, 2004.

4   Mildred Constantine, interview, January 11, 2007.

5   Bill Freeman, email, July 29, 2008

6   Evan Eckerstrom, email, June 11, 2007.

7   Alan Heller, interview, June 14, 2012.

8   Simon Jennings, email, August 25, 2009.

9   Ted Peterson, interview, December 20, 2006.

10 William Plumb, ed., "An Exchange of Views: Order vs. Disorder—and Some Related Matters," *Print* (March/April 1968), p. 81.

11 Ibid., p. 83.

12 Michael Donovan, interview, June 14, 2012.

13 Seiler and Kirkham, "Lella Vignelli on Vignelli: Design History, Concepts, and Collaboration," *Studies in the Decorative Arts.* (Fall–Winter 2000–2001), p. 148.

14 Michael Donovan, email, July 19, 2013.

15 Heinz Waibl, interview, September 28, 2006.

16 Katherine McCoy, email, August 8, 2006.

17 Grant Smith, email, August 12, 2006.

18 Peter Teubner, interview, December 27, 2006.

19 Bill Freeman, email, July 29, 2008.

20 Joel Margulies, interview, January 10, 2007.

21 David Law, interview, March 14, 1988.

22 Jan von Holstein, interview, July 13, 2004.

23 Harri Boller, interview, December 15, 2006.

1971: The Rise of Vignelli Associates

1   "Introduction, The Vignellis: Profile of a Design Team," *ID* (1981), p. 9.

2   Michael Donovan, interview, June 14, 2012.

3   Martin Filler, "Leaving It Better Than They Found It," *Progressive Architecture* (September 1978), p. 102.

4   Michael Bierut, interview, February 1, 2013.

5   Laura Hillyer, interview, July 9, 2012.

6   Lanny Sommese, "Symbol Signs," *Novum Gebrauchs Graphik,* volume 48 (June 1977), p. 22.

7   Beatriz Cifuentes and Yoshiki Waterhouse, eds., *Massimo 80th Birthday,* privately published, 2011.

8   Ibid.

9   Saint Peter's Church, "Vignelli Design: A Powerful, Elegant, Timeless Approach to Church," www.saintpeters.org/the-arts-and-design/vignelli-design/ (accessed August 7, 2013).

10 Michael Donovan, interview, June 14, 2012.

11 Yoshimi Kono, interview, September 14, 2013.

12 Sharon Singer, interview, September 13, 2013.

13 Lev Zeitlin, interview, July 6, 2013.

14 Ibid.

15 Caterina Roiatti, interview, February 2, 2013.

16 Laura Hillyer, interview, July 9, 2012.

17 Michael Donovan, interview, June 14, 2012.

18 Lev Zeitlin, interview, July 6, 2013.

19 Laura Hillyer, interview, July 9, 2012.

20 Norma Skurka, "Spare Is More," *New York Times* (April 20, 1975), pp. 92–93.

21 Steven Holt, "Vignelli and Glaser Square off on the Dimension Question." *ID* (May/June 1983), pp. 14–15.

22 Bill Freeman, email, August 3, 2008.

23 Michael Bierut, interview, February 1, 2013.

24 Jonathan Wajskol, interview, June 29, 2011.

25 Michael Donovan, interview, March 8, 1988.

26 Graham Hanson, email, July 29, 2013.

27 Sharon Singer, interview, September 13, 2013.

28 Cifuentes and Waterhouse, eds., *Massimo 80th Birthday*.

29 Yoshiki Waterhouse, interview, May 11, 2011.

30 Lev Zeitlin, interview, July 6, 2013.

31 Robert Traboscia, interview, January 17, 2013.

32 Sharon Singer, interview, September 13, 2013.

33 Michael Bierut, *Seventy-nine Short Essays on Design* (New York: Princeton Architectural Press, 2007), p. 242.

34 Rocco Piscatello, interview, July 21, 2013.

35 Seiler and Kirkham, "Lella Vignelli on Vignelli," p. 152.

The Showcase Office: Tenth Avenue

1 Paul M. Sachner, "The Lords of Discipline." *Architectural Record* (September 1986), p. 122.

2 Rocco Piscatello, interview, January 10, 2011.

3 Yoshimi Kono, interview, September 14, 2013.

4 Sharon Singer, interview, September 13, 2013.

5 Cifuentes and Waterhouse, eds., *Massimo 80th Birthday*.

6 Willam P. Dunk, "Design & Business." *Graphis* (November 1990), p. 12.

7 *Print Regional Design Annual* (July/August 1991), p. 51

8 Yoshimi Kono, interview, September 14, 2013.

9 Janice Carapellucci, interview, July 12, 2013.

10 Cifuentes and Waterhouse, eds., *Massimo 80th Birthday*.

11 Samira Bouabana and Angela Tillman Sperandio, *Hall of Femmes: Lella Vignelli* (Stockholm: Oyster Press, 2013), p. 59.

12   Andrew Olds, "Design Vignelli: Ready-to-Wear in Ten Pieces or Less." *ID* (Sept./ Oct. 1991), p. 9.

13   Nancy Olnick and Giorgio Spanu, interview, August 11, 2013.

14   J. Peter Pawlak, "Currents: Manhattan Space; With Rents as High as the Skyline, Designers Seek a New Home." *The New York Times*. (September 28, 2000).

15   Sharon Singer, interview, September 13, 2013.

16   Jonathan Wajskol, interview, June 29, 2012.

17   Michael Bierut, email, July 10, 2013.

18   Michael Bierut, "Battle Hymn of the Tiger Mentor, Or, Why Modernist Designers Are Superior," *Design Observer* (January 31, 2011). http://observatory. designobserver.com/entry.html?entry=24558 (accessed November 21, 2013).

19   Rocco Piscatello, interview, August 29, 2010

Working from Home: East 67th Street

1   Michael Donovan, interview, June 14, 2012.

2   Michael Bierut, interview, February 1, 2013.

3   Yoshiki Waterhouse, interview, July 6, 2013.

4   Caterina Roiatti, interview, February 2, 2013.

5   Edie Cohen, "Artemide, Miami: The Vignelli Associates' Showroom in the Design Center of the Americas," *Interior Design* (June 1987), p. 240.

6   Jen Renzi, "100 Percent Pure Italian," *Interior Design* (May 2003), p. 98.

7   Graham Hanson, email, July 29, 2013.

8   Beatriz Cifuentes and Yoshiki Waterhouse, interview, July 6, 2013

9   Designboom, "NYC Subway Diagram 2008 by Massimo Vignelli for Men's Vogue," http://www.designboom.com/design/nyc-subway-diagram-2008-by-massimo-vignelli-for-mens-vogue/ (accessed August 7, 2013).

10   Peter Lloyd, *Vignelli Transit Maps* (Rochester: RIT Cary Graphic Arts Press, 2012), p. 100.

11   *The New Yorker,* "The Vignelli Subway Map Goes Digital," Paul Goldberger, September 23, 2011, http://www.newyorker.com/online/blogs/newsdesk/2011/09/ vignelli-subway-map-mta.html (accessed August 7, 2013). Experience Alexander Chen's musical subway map at http://www.mta.me (accessed January 15, 2014).

12   *Fast Company,* "The Science of a Great Subway Map," Eric Jaffe, October 29, 2013, http://www.fastcodesign.com/3020708/evidence/the-science-of-a-great-subway-map (accessed November 21, 2013).

Design Advocacy

1   Donald Meeker, letter to Lella Vignelli, June 5, 1989 (Vignelli Archives).

2   Lella Vignelli, memo to Robert Feely at Shearman & Sterling, November 24, 1986 (Vignelli Archives).

3   Rocco Piscatello, interview, August 29, 2010.

4   Ivan Chermayeff, interview, February 18, 2011.

5   Massimo Vignelli, *Grids: Their Meaning and Use for Federal Designers* (Washington, D.C.: U.S. Government Printing Office, December 1978). This document can be viewed at https://archive.org/details/gridstheirmeanin00vign

6   From an undated eighteen-page document (Massimo said it was written by Vincent Gleason). It has a cover note that Massimo wrote to his staff: "This letter should be mandatory reading for everybody in the office. It shows the relevance of working for public interest." (Vignelli Archives)

7   Ibid.

8   For a clear description of the structure of the Unigrid, see Rob Carter, Ben Day, Phillip Meggs, *Typographic Design: Form and Communication* (New York: John J. Wiley & Sons, Inc.)

9   Unigrid Design Specifications (Vignelli Archives)

10 Ibid.

11 From the Gleason document (Vignelli Archives). See note 6.

12 Massimo Vignelli, *"The Design Profession: Where We Are/Where We Are Going."* Text of speech presented to Icograda Congress, Eindhoven, The Netherlands. August 1968.

13 George Nelson, "Design on a Small Planet," *ID* (Nov./Dec. 1983), p. 11.

14 Michael Kroeger, *Paul Rand: Conversations with Students* (New York: Princeton Architectural Press, 2008), p. 52.

15 *The First Symposium of the History of Graphic Design: Coming of Age* (conference documentation printed by Rochester Institute of Technology in 1983), p. 11.

16 Janice Carapellucci, interview, July 12, 2013.

17 Paul Rand, *Paul Rand: A Designer's Art* (New Haven: Yale University Press, 1985), p. 234.

18 *Vanity Fair,* "Something Lousy in the Air: Analyzing American Airlines' Disastrous Redesign," Paul Goldberger, January 22, 2013, http://www.vanityfair.com/online/daily/2013/01/analyzing-american-airlines-disastrous-redesign (accessed August 7, 2013).

19 Massimo Vignelli, letter to Laurie Haycock Makela, June 22, 1993 (Vignelli Archives).

20 Steven Heller, letter to Massimo, July 4, 1990 (Vignelli Archives).

21 Massimo Vignelli, "Long Live Modernism!" *AIGA Journal of Graphic Design,* vol. 9, no. 2 (1991), p. 1.

22 Philip B. Meggs, "The Obscene Typography Machine." Print (Sept./Oct. 1989).

23 Rocco Piscatello, email, January 16, 2014.

24 "Oppositions: Massimo Vignelli vs. Ed Benguiat (Sort Of)," *Print* (Sept./Oct. 1991), pp. 88–95.

25 Massimo Vignelli, letter to AGI/IEC members, August 18, 1988 (Vignelli Archives).

26 Massimo Vignelli, "From Less Is More to Less Is a Bore. Is More the Better?" *U&lc* (December 1982), p. 10.

27 Massimo Vignelli, "La New York Dei Vignelli (The Vignellis' New York)." *Domus 972* (September 2013), pp. 148–149.

28 Memo with text of Furio Colombo speech, November 6, 1992 (Vignelli Archives).

29 Lella Vignelli, letter to Joan Mondale, July 31, 1984 (Vignelli Archives).

30 Massimo Vignelli, letter to Charles Orlebeke, March 10, 1992 (Vignelli Archives).

31 Bouabana and Sperandio, *Hall of Femmes: Lella Vignelli.* p. 30.

32 Ibid., p. 57.

33 Robert Swinehart, interview, July 25, 2013.

Students, Teaching, and Learning

1 Massimo Vignelli, *The Vignelli Canon.* (Baden, Lars Müller Publishers, 2010), p. 4

2 Jean Taylor, letter to Massimo Vignelli, April 9, 1986 (Vignelli Archives).

3 Massimo was referring to the architects Robert Adam and Charles Rennie Mackintosh. Robert Adam, his brothers James and John, and his father William were all architects. Both Adam and Mackintosh worked to unite architectural exteriors, interiors, and furnishings into unified designs.

4 Massimo Vignelli, letter to Jean Taylor, September 8, 1986 (Vignelli Archives).

5 Seiler and Kirkham, "Lella Vignelli on Vignelli," p. 151.

6 RIT, "Grand Opening and Dedication of Vignelli Center for Design Studies Sept. 16," Kelly Downs, September 9, 2010, http://www.rit.edu/news/story.php?id=47784 (accessed August 7, 2013).

A Lifetime, and No Regrets

1 Robert Swinehart, interview, July 25, 2013.

2 George Lois, interview, June 24, 2013.

3 Ashraf Elfiky, email, July 29, 2010.

4 Sean Wolcott, interview, July 26, 2013.

5 Michael Gagliano, interview, July 26, 2013.

6 Caterina Roiatti, interview, February 2, 2013.

7 Massimo Vignelli, letter to George Haessler, November 3, 1987 (Vignelli Archives).

8 Beatriz Cifuentes and Yoshiki Waterhouse, interview, July 6, 2013

9 Ibid.

10 Alan Heller, interview, June 14, 2012.

11 Nancy Olnick and Giorgio Spanu, interview, August 11, 2013.

12 Ibid.

13 Antonio Capaldo, email, July 10, 2013

14 Stan Pinkwas, "King and Queen of Cups," *Metropolis* (January 1983), p. 17.

1. Massimo, age 11, 1942
2. Massimo with his mother, in Genoa, 1942
3. Massimo with his father, 1931
4. At 10 months, November 1932
5. Massimo in Pegli, Italy, 1939

1

2

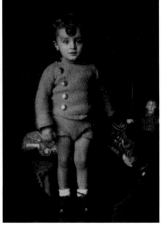

3

4

5

6

7

8   9

136

1. *Massimo working in Venice, 1956*
2. *Massimo, self-portrait, 1953*
3. *Lella, 1951*
4. *Lella on the mountainside, undated photo*

1

2

3

4

5. *Lella in Venice, 1955*
6. *Massimo and Lella with classmates, in Venice, circa 1954*
7.. *Massimo in Venice, 1953*
8. *Massimo on the stairs in Siena, 1949*

5

6

7, 8

1

2

3

4

1. *Massimo and Lella on their wedding day, September 15, 1957, with Paolo Venini*
2. *Ralph Eckerstrom, Wally Gutches, and Massimo at Unimark International, 1967*
3. *Design jury with Henry Wolf, Milton Glaser, Massimo, 1973*
4. *Lella at work, 1980*

5.   *Lella with Luca and Valentina,
     circa 1969*
6.   *The Vignellis at home, 1972*
7.   *Lella and Valentina, 1976*

5

6

7

1. *Michael Bierut with the Vignellis, 1984*
2. *With Ivan Chermayeff at the AIGA Gold Medal Awards Ceremony, 1983*
3. *Alliance Graphique Internationale (AGI) meeting in Zurich, September 1986.*
   Left to right: Gene Frederico, Ralph Müller, Fritz Gottschalk, Massimo,
   Rudi Ruegg, Takeo Igarashi
4. *Lella and Luca, 1984*

5

5. *A devilishly good time at a Vignelli Associates Halloween party, circa 1987*
    Back: A Sasaki representative, (?), Alan Hopfensperger, Barbara Genova,
    Massimo as the devil, Michael Leone, Denise Czar, Douglas Frueh, Laura Hillyer
    Middle: Lella, Rebecca Rose, Janice Carapellucci, Mark Randall,
    Sharon Singer, Patty White, Donesia Morris, Matilde Chacon
    Front: Sarah Riegelmann, David Law, Yoshimi Kono, Jenny Murphy,
    Margareth Innerhofer

1. *Lella and Gae Aulenti in Milan, 2000*
2. *R.Roger Remington and Massimo, lecturing at RIT, 2013*
3. *Lella and R.Roger Remington at RIT, 2010*
4. *Massimo working with Dante O. Benini, 2007*

1

2

A. Sue Weisler

3

4

5. *Lella and Massimo at RIT, 2010*
6. *Armando Milani, the Vignellis, Cynthia Milani, R. Roger Remington, France, 2010*
7. *Massimo explaining grid structure at the master designer workshop in France, 2010*

5

6

7

1

2

1. *The Vignelli Center for Design Studies at RIT*
2. *Lella and Beatriz Cifuentes preparing
   exhibits in the Benetton Gallery at RIT, 2010*
3. *Former Vignelli Associates: Graham Hanson,
   Beatriz Cifuentes, Yoshiki Waterhouse,
   Massimo Vignelli, Rocco Piscatello,
   Alessandro Franchini, Lella Vignelli,
   Michael Bierut, Michael Donovan*

3

1. Assembling gallery displays at RIT, 2010
2–8. At the dedication ceremonies for the Vignelli Center, September 2010
9. Valentina, Luca, Lella at the ceremonies
10. Ceremonial ribbon-cutting: RIT President Dr. William W. Destler, Lady Helen Hamlyn, Lella, Massimo, (R. Roger Remington watching)

4

5

Elizabeth Lamark, RIT Production Services

6

7

8

9

A. Sue Weisler

10

A. Sue Weisler

1

A. Sue Weisler

2

3

1. *Massimo explaining the National Park Service system to RIT students, 2010*
2. *Students at the master designer workshop in the Vignelli Center, 2013*
3. *Massimo working at home*
4. *Massimo and Lella Vignelli at their home in New York, Oct. 11, 2012.*

4

"The life of a designer is a life of fight:
fight against the ugliness."

Afterword

On May 27, 2014, after difficult final months of frustrating medical issues, Massimo Vignelli passed away quietly at home. Lella Vignelli remains in the Vignelli home with the help of caretakers and family.

A notable passing inevitably leads to thoughts of legacy and influence. Massimo Vignelli's most meaningful legacy was relationships. He was a designer—a builder—not simply of materials, but of ideas and of people. Massimo focused, listened, shared, and cared. His steadfast commitment to an ideal world that could never be realized, to the purpose of bettering society, and to a process of thinking and doing toward these ends lasted through his lifetime. His influence is lasting because he inspired countless others to continue in this positive direction.

Having Vignelli credentials opened doors for dozens of designers; railing against Vignelli vision bolstered recognition for others. Only a great visionary could have it both ways. Even those who criticized his design approach readily admitted appreciation of him; Massimo was personally likeable even when his tongue was sharp. His impassioned embrace of an engaged life came with a ready smile, quick wit, raised eyebrows and a nimble mind.

Criticism by Massimo had poetic sting. Neither friendship nor professional respect were insulators when his observations could be forcefully delivered in two languages—his eloquence in English matched his fluidity in Italian. His critical appraisal always focused on ideas or execution that failed his test of integrity and meaning. At the same time, earning his praise felt as though you'd personally contributed to his constant battle against mediocrity, obsolescence, and the consequent deterioration of society itself.

Personally, I will miss his "Massimoisms" that played so fluently with language. Some of them were repeated for decades, others were off-the-cuff quips, but all of them were meaningful. His expressiveness put people at ease, made them think, and offered easy entrance to difficult topics.

Upon learning that I was raised on an Iowa Holstein farm, his response was instantaneous. "Iowa is one large grid, and with black and white cows too, *you had to become a graphic designer*," he told me. In 1978, the Icograda Congress met in Evanston, Illinois. Massimo was one of the speakers and he criticized the organization of a conference presentation that was too one-sided, saying, "I want to hear both bells, and then decide which has the most silvery sound." A 2013 video created for Mohawk paper, *Massimo Vignelli Makes Books*, showed him explaining the grid. "The grid is an integral part of book design. It's not something that you see. It's just like underwear: you wear it, but it's not to be exposed. The grid is the underwear of the book."

These observations continued even in the last weeks of his life. When shown an x-ray of a his spine, eroding from a recurrent infection, he soberly pondered the visual evidence. "It looks like a rat chewed a hole in my spine," he said. He drew a quick sketch of the offending beast with a shaky hand.

Integrity was a favorite word for both Massimo and Lella Vignelli. It defined them. Few people sustained and blended work and life with such assurance and success. Massimo found joy in the good things of life, in the beauty of smooth functionality, in honesty of materials and careful craftsmanship. During his last hospital stay, he wanted his ginger ale iced in a bucket like champagne and though it was more difficult for him to maneuver, he insisted that Luca straighten his bedside table to a proper 90-degree angle before he would eat. Massimo was orderly to the end.

Until recently Massimo proclaimed that he would like to live forever, to keep working forever. When facing the end, his biggest concern was protecting and providing for Lella. He did not fear death itself, but he worried that in passing he would become that most reviled entity—a transient being. Massimo detested things that were ephemeral. That focus led him to a lifetime of teaching, sharing, and explaining ideas and methods with consistency, clarity, and patience to clients and designers alike. Through the relationships he fostered, he will do as he wanted—he will live forever.

Near the end, son Luca did his best to make his father happy, which usually meant keeping him focused on the world of design. Luca issued a request for letters from those who felt Massimo's influence. Through social media, his request quickly went viral. In the final days of Massimo's life, hundreds of messages poured in, some witty, some serious; all expressing gratitude and support to him—to the mentor who touched their lives and work in a meaningful way.

In 1977, the Vignellis designed the interior of St. Peter's Church in New York City. In 1994, Massimo and Lella were officially honored with a niche in the columbarium as their eventual final resting place. In a letter to the Pastor and the congregation, Massimo wrote, "There is no place in the world where we would like to rest more than St. Peter's Church, a place we designed with love and respect."

With love and respect, I offer this book as a tribute to Massimo and Lella Vignelli.

Appendix: Awards and Accolades

The Vignellis' work has been included in the permanent collections of several museums, notably the Museum of Modern Art, The Metropolitan Museum of Art, the Cooper-Hewitt Museum, and the Brooklyn Museum in New York; the Victoria and Albert Museum in London; the Musée des Arts Decoratifs in Montreal; and the Die Neue Sammlung in Munich.

They have been the subject of multiple videos; a 2012 feature-length film, *Design Is One: Massimo & Lella Vignelli;* and two television programs, *The Artist Toolbox: Massimo & Lella Vignelli* in 2011, and *Interior Design: The New Freedom: Massimo and Lella Vignelli* in 1981. A monographic exhibition of the Vignellis' work toured Europe between 1989 and 1993, and was featured in Barcelona, Budapest, Copenhagen, Helsinki, London, Moscow, Munich, Paris, Prague, and St. Petersburg.

Shared Vignelli Awards

1973	Industrial Arts Medal, American Institute of Architects (AIA)
1982	Honorary doctorate in fine arts, Parsons School of Design, New York
1983	Gold Medal, AIGA
1988	Interior Design Hall of Fame
1991	Gold Medal for Design, National Arts Club
1992	Interior Product Designers Fellowship of Excellence
1994	Honorary doctorate in fine arts, Corcoran School of Art, Washington, D.C.
1995	Design Award for Lifetime Achievement, Brooklyn Museum
1996	Honorary Royal Designer for Industry Award, Royal Society of Arts, London
2003	National Lifetime Achievement Award, National Museum of Design at Cooper-Hewitt, New York
2004	Visionary Award, Museum of Art and Design, New York
2005	Architecture Award, American Academy of Arts and Letters, New York
2011	President's Medal, Architectural League of New York
2014	Il Ponte, Fondazione Europea Guido Venosta, Milan, Italy

Lella Vignelli

Lella Vignelli is the subject of a 2013 monograph, *Hall of Femmes: Lella Vignelli* (Stockholm: Oyster Press, 2013). Her work has been widely featured in design publications in the United States and abroad. She has been a frequent speaker and juror for national and international design organizations. She is a member of the American Institute of Graphic Arts (AIGA), the Decorators Club of New York, the Industrial Designers Society of America (IDSA), and the International Furnishings and Designer Association (IFDA).

Massimo Vignelli

Massimo Vignelli is a past president of the Alliance Graphique Internationale (AGI) and the American Institute of Graphic Arts (AIGA), a vice president of the Architectural League, and a member of the Industrial Designers Society of America (IDSA). His work, his writings, and his interviews have been published worldwide. He has taught and lectured on design in major universities and cities in the United States and abroad.

Massimo Vignelli's many awards include:

1964	Gran Premio Triennale di Milano.
1964	Compasso d'Oro, Italian Association for Industrial Design (ADI)
1982	New York Art Directors Club Hall of Fame
1985	The first Presidential Design Award, presented by President Ronald Reagan, for the National Park Service Publications Program
1987	Honorary doctorate in fine arts, Pratt Institute, Brooklyn, New York
1988	Honorary doctorate in fine arts, Rhode Island School of Design, Providence, Rhode Island
1991	Masters Series Award, School of Visual Arts, New York
1993	New York State Governor's Award for Excellence
1994	Honorary doctorate in architecture from the University of Venice, Italy
1998	Compasso d'Oro, Italian Association for Industrial Design (ADI)
2000	Honorary doctorate in fine arts, Art Center College of Design, Pasadena, California
2002	Honorary doctorate in fine arts, Rochester Institute of Technology, Rochester, New York

Index

Colophon

Design
Jan Conradi

Production
Marnie Soom

Typefaces
Helvetica Neue and Minion Pro

Printing and binding
Thomson-Shore, Inc., Dexter, MI

Paper
80 lb. Huron Gloss